P9-ELS-500

PRINTING PRESS

Ideas into Type

These and other books are included in the
Encyclopedia of Discovery and Invention
series:

Airplanes: The Lure of Flight
Atoms: Building Blocks of Matter
Computers: Mechanical Minds
Gravity: The Universal Force
Lasers: Humanity's Magic Light
Printing Press: Ideas into Type
Radar: The Silent Detector
Television: Electronic Pictures

PRINTING PRESS

Ideas into Type

by BRADLEY STEFFENS

The ENCYCLOPEDIA of
D·I·S·C·O·V·E·R·Y
and INVENTION

Lucent Books, P.O. Box 289011 SAN DIEGO, CA 92198 0011

Library of Congress Cataloging-in-Publication Data

Steffens, Bradley, 1956–
    The printing press: ideas into type/by Bradley Steffens.
        p. cm.— (Encyclopedia of discovery and invention)
    Includes bibliographical references and index.
    Summary: Discusses the invention of mechanical printing, from its
origins in China through Gutenberg to present technology, examining
typography, graphic arts, paper, bookbinding, photography, and the
cultural contexts of printing.
    ISBN 1-56006-205-3
    1. Printing-press—History—Juvenile literature. 2. Printing—
History—Juvenile literature. [1. Printing.] [I.] Title.
II. Series.
Z249.S823 1990
686.2—dc20   90-6619

Contents

■ ■

Foreword

The belief in progress has been one of the dominant forces in Western Civilization from the Scientific Revolution of the seventeenth century to the present. Embodied in the idea of progress is the conviction that each generation will be better off than the one that preceded it. Eventually, all peoples will benefit from and share in this better world. R. R. Palmer, in his *History of the Modern World*, calls this belief in progress "a kind of nonreligious faith that the conditions of human life" will continually improve as time goes on.

For over a thousand years prior to the seventeenth century, science had progressed little. Inquiry was largely discouraged, and experimentation almost nonexistent. As a result, science became regressive and discovery was ignored. Benjamin Farrington, a historian of science, characterized it this way: "Science had failed to become a real force in the life of society. Instead there had arisen a conception of science as a cycle of liberal studies for a privileged minority. Science ceased to be a means of transforming the conditions of life." In short, had this intellectual climate continued, humanity's future world would have been little more than a clone of its past.

Fortunately, these circumstances were not destined to last. By the seventeenth and eighteenth centuries, Western society was undergoing radical and favorable changes. And the changes that occurred gave rise to the notion that progress was a real force urging civilization forward. Surpluses of consumer goods were replacing substandard living conditions in most of Western Europe. Rigid class systems were giving way to social mobility. In nations like France and the United States, the lofty principles of democracy and popular sovereignty were being painted in broad, gilded strokes over the fading canvasses of monarchy and despotism.

But more significant than these social, economic, and political changes, the new age witnessed a rebirth of science. Centuries of scientific stagnation began crumbling before a spirit of scientific inquiry that spawned undreamed of technological advances. And it was the discoveries and inventions of scores of men and women that fueled these new technologies, dramatically increasing the ability of humankind to control nature—and, many believed, eventually to guide it.

It is a truism of science and technology that the results derived from observation and experimentation are not finalities. They are part of a process. Each discovery is but one piece in a continuum bridging past and present and heralding an extraordinary future. The heroic age of the Scientific Revolution was simply a start. It laid a foundation upon which succeeding generations of imaginative thinkers could build. It kindled the belief that progress is possible as long as there were gifted men and women who would respond to society's needs. When Antonie van Leeuwenhoek observed *Animalcules* (little animals) through his high-powered microscope in 1683, the discovery did not end there. Others followed who would call these "little animals" bacteria and, in time, recognize their role in the process of health and disease. Robert Koch, a German bacteriologist and winner of the Nobel prize in Physiology and Medicine, was one of these men. Koch firmly established that bacteria are responsible for causing infectious diseases. He identified, among others, the causative organisms of anthrax and tuberculosis. Alexander Fleming, another Nobel Laureate, progressed still further in the quest to understand and control bacteria. In 1928, Fleming discovered penicillin, the antibiotic wonder drug. Penicillin, and the generations of antibiotics that succeeded it, have done more to prevent premature death than any other discovery in the history of humankind. And as civilization hastens toward the twenty-first century, most agree that the conquest of van Leeuwenhoek's "little animals" will continue.

The *Encyclopedia of Discovery and Invention* examines those discoveries and inventions that have had a sweeping impact on life and thought in the modern world. Each book explores the ideas that led to the invention or discovery, and, more importantly, how the world changed and continues to change because of it. The series also highlights the people behind the achievements—the unique men and women whose singular genius and rich imagination have altered the lives of everyone. Enhanced by photographs and clearly explained technical drawings, these books are comprehensive examinations of the building blocks of human progress.

PRINTING PRESS

Ideas into Type

PRINTING PRESS

Introduction

This printed page has a story behind it. It is the history of paper, ink, and the machine that brings these two materials together: the printing press. It is a story of hard work and brilliant ingenuity, of visionary kings, devoted priests, and grasping businessmen. It is a story that is nearly two thousand years old. It begins in China in A.D. 105.

By the first century A.D., the Chinese had learned the basic process of printing: the transferring of permanent image-making materials—like ink, paint, or dye—from one surface onto another.

The Chinese used this process to decorate fabric. In A.D. 105, a Chinese inventor named Ts'ai Lun invented a new material, known as paper, that changed the course of printing.

Once people began to experiment with printing on paper, the art of printing as we know it was born. Communication became the most important function of printing, and printing became the world's most important form of communication.

Printing made the duplication of writings easier and faster. As a result, the insights and knowledge of leaders and thinkers could be spread much more

TIMELINE: PRINTING PRESS

1 ■ 105
Ts'ai Lun invents paper.

2 ■ 210
Wei Tan creates permanent ink.

3 ■ 618
Buddhist priests blockprint on paper.

4 ■ 868
The first printed book, The *Diamond Sutra*, completed.

5 ■ 1041
Pi Sheng invents movable type.

6 ■ 1438
Johannes Gutenberg forms partnership to develop printing press.

7 ■ 1446
Sejong the Great orders the creation of a Korean alphabet so more books can be printed with movable type.

8 ■ 1456
John Fust and Peter Schöffer complete work on the Gutenberg Bible, the first book printed in Europe with movable type.

9 ■ 1461
Albrecht Pfister publishes first typeset book written in the vernacular. Book includes first illustrations used with movable type.

10 ■ 1465
Sweynheym and Pannartz publish *Opera* by Lactantius, first book printed in roman type.

11 ■ 1493
Ferdinand and Isabella order newsbook printed telling of voyage of Christopher Columbus.

12 ■ 1609
Johann Carolus and Lucas Schulte produce first newspapers.

13 ■ 1641
Samuel Pecke defies British law against publishing news about the monarchy.

quickly. These ideas changed how people thought about themselves, their religions, and their leaders. These changing attitudes led to changes in society. In short, printing helped change the world.

Many of the greatest changes occurred after a German inventor named Johannes Gutenberg refined the process of printing around 1438. Gutenberg hired a woodworker named Conrad Saspach to build a press that was similar to presses used to crush olives and grapes. Gutenberg wanted to press an inked surface against paper. When Saspach delivered the device to Gutenberg, the invention of the printing press itself was complete.

Gutenberg's press was not the most important advancement in the history of printing, however. It was not even the most important contribution Gutenberg made to the art of printing. His greatest achievement was conceiving and perfecting a method of printing using small metal letters, known as movable type. But even this method of printing was eventually replaced by other methods. The printing press is not a single invention, but many different inventions. The history of printing is not the story of one person, but of many.

It is a story that continues to be written today.

14 ⟩ 15 ⟩ 16 ⟩ 17 ⟩ 18 ⟩ 19 ⟩ 20 ⟩ 21 ⟩ 22 ⟩ 23 ⟩ 24 ⟩ 25 ⟩ 26 ⟩ 27 ⟩ 28 ⟩

14 ■ 1690
Benjamin Harris publishes first newspaper in the American colonies.

15 ■ 1789
First U.S. Congress guarantees freedom of the press.

16 ■ 1790
William Nicholson designs stop-cylinder press.

17 ■ 1796
Alois Senefelder discovers lithography.

18 ■ 1800
Charles, Earl of Stanhope, completes first all-metal press.

19 ■ 1812
Frederick Konig invents first steam-powered press.

20 ■ 1835
W. H. Fox Talbot and Louis Daguerre invent photography.

21 ■ 1852
Talbot invents half tone processing.

22 ■ 1880
First half-tone engraving published in newspaper.

23 ■ 1893
Color processing invented.

24 ■ 1906
Ira Rubel and A. F. Harris invent off-set printing.

25 ■ 1920
First phototypesetter built.

26 ■ 1937
First xerographic printer invented by Chester Caslon.

27 ■ 1960
Xerox Corporation introduces first commercial xerographic copier.

28 ■ 1985
Apple Corporation introduces Laserwriter, first commercial laser printer.

First compact disk information storage and retrieval system introduced.

The Origin of Printing

Dressed in his finest silk robe, Ts'ai Lun made his way through the halls of the Emperor Ho's great palace in A.D.105. In his hands, Ts'ai Lun carried a remarkable new material that was ideal for writing on. It was flatter, stiffer, than silk, the material on which Han Dynasty scribes recorded official documents, and it absorbed ink better. It was easier to store, and, best of all, cheaper to produce. In fact, it was made from nothing more than scraps and trash.

Workers collect scraps and trash to be boiled into a thick goo for paper.

Ts'ai Lun spread the thick goo of scraps and trash in a thin layer across a bamboo screen and then placed the material in the sun to dry. The material dried into a stiff sheet, but could be folded without breaking.

To make the new material, Ts'ai Lun had boiled mulberry bark, hemp, rags, and old fishnets together in a pot. He had mashed the softened materials into a thick goo, then spread the substance in a thin layer across a bamboo screen. He placed the material in the sun to dry. As moisture seeped through the bamboo screen and evaporated into the air, the material dried into a stiff sheet. Ts'ai Lun's heart raced as he carried this sheet toward the throne room.

Using block printing, one man could produce about 2,000 printed pages a day.

A worker boils mulberry bark in a wooden barrel to make paper.

He was about to present this new invention—paper—to the emperor himself.

Ts'ai Lun explained to Emperor Ho that the new substance made an ideal writing material. He demonstrated how it absorbed ink, and how if folded without breaking. Two hundred years before, silk had replaced bamboo strips for the recording of official documents. Now paper seemed destined to replace silk. Emperor Ho praised Ts'ai Lun for his achievement. He ordered the inventor to teach others how to make the extraordinary material.

In the years that followed, the art of papermaking spread across all of China. One of those who learned the process from Ts'ai Lun was a young calligrapher named Tso Po. Tso Po found many ways to improve upon Ts'ai Lun's invention. Tso Po's refinements were so great that a Chinese man named Hsiao Tzu-liang wrote to a friend, "The paper of Tso Po, together with his ink and brushes, is especially fine; none can reach their degree of excellence."

Paper sheets dry on a wall and are heated by a primitive stove.

Chinese inventors also worked at improving ink. In the third century, a Chinese inventor named Wei Tan mixed oil with the soot from lamps blackened by burning to make a fine, durable ink The oil made the ink thick and easy to work with. The soot made it dark and virtually permanent. Lampblack, composed mainly of carbon, decays slowly, so an ink made with it lasts a very long time.

As the knowledge of papermaking spread across China, people from every walk of life found new uses for the amazing material. By the eighth century, the Chinese were using paper to make everything from wall coverings to toilet paper.

Block Printing

During the Han Dynasty, which lasted from 207 B.C. to A.D. 220, the Chinese people followed many different philosophies and practiced several different religions, including Confucianism, Taoism, and Buddhism. But it was Buddhism that would influence the earliest form of true printing.

Buddhism was founded around sixth century B.C. by a priest and teacher named Gautama Siddhartha, whose followers called him the Buddha, meaning "the enlightened one." The Buddha taught that enlightenment, or nirvana, is reached by a combination of belief, right living, and meditation.

Some of the earliest experiments with printing were performed by Buddhist priests in an act of devotion. The followers of Gautama Siddhartha believe him to be the last in a series of divine teachers. Buddhists believe that because the Buddha is an incarnation of God, reproducing his image is a sacred act. As a sign of devotion, ancient Chinese Buddhists carved the Buddha's figure into wood, stone, and ivory and placed these figures in their temples and homes.

By the fifth century, Buddhist priests had found a number of ways that paper could be used to reproduce the image of the Buddha. They discovered that if they placed a sheet of paper over a carving of the Buddha and rubbed the surface with chalk, particles of the chalk would catch on the raised points of the carving, leaving an image of the

A depiction of early Chinese block-printing techniques shows one man carving a woodblock. The other man coats the woodblock with ink, presses a piece of rice paper against it and then moves a brush over the paper.

Buddha on the paper. This process is known as taking a rubbing.

Buddhists also found that they could cut a hole in a sheet of paper in the shape of the Buddha, then hold the paper against a wall and paint over it. The paint would fill in the cutout shape of the Buddha, leaving his image on the surface. This process is known as stenciling. Buddhist priests continued to experiment with replicating Buddha's image. In fact, historian Daniel J. Boorstin claims that this "duplicating impulse" was the driving force behind the Buddhists' discovery of the first known form of printing with paper and ink.

During the Tang Dynasty, which ruled China from A.D. 618 to 907, priests carved Buddha's likeness on a flat piece of wood, then coated the carving with ink. When they pressed the inked surface against a piece of paper, the image of the Buddha was transferred to the paper. This process is known as block printing, and it is the earliest form of printing known to exist.

While block printing had been used in China for centuries to decorate fabric with shapes and designs, printing on paper was undertaken for an entirely different reason. The purpose of printing on fabric was to decorate the cloth. Printing on paper was also used to produce decoration, but its main purpose was to remind the viewer of the importance of the Buddha. The goal was communication, not simply decoration.

Soon Buddhist priests began adding words to their block prints of the Buddha. Printed pages included not only the image of the Buddha but also his sayings and teachings.

By the eighth century, both the Buddhist religion and the art of block printing had spread to Japan. In 735, a

A late eighteenth-century block print shows two women in a traditional Chinese scene.

smallpox epidemic struck Japan, taking the lives of many people, including members of the royal court. After the Empress Shōkotu, a devout Buddhist, came to power in 749, she ordered that twenty-five lines of sacred Buddhist text be printed on one million sheets of paper. These sheets were then placed inside small, carved pagodas as charms against the recurrence of the smallpox epidemic. These charms, completed around 770, are among the earliest examples of printing on paper in existence today.

The First Printed Books

About one hundred years later, a Chinese printer named Wang Chieh began reproducing the Buddha's teachings in earnest. Wang Chieh collected several of the Buddha's sermons and printed them using block printing on six sheets of paper, each of which was twelve inches high and thirty inches long. Wang Chieh's printers glued these

The followers of Confucius, a sixth-century Chinese teacher and philosopher, used block printing to pass on the wisdom of their teacher.

sheets together, end to end, along with a seventh, shorter sheet bearing a woodcut illustration, to make a scroll. According to Wang Chieh's inscription, this collection, known as *The Diamond Sutra,* was completed on May 11, 868. It is the world's oldest surviving printed book.

Buddhist priests were not the only religious leaders who recognized the value of block printing. The followers of Confucius, a sixth-century Chinese teacher and philosopher, also began to print the sayings of their teacher on paper.

The process was slow and painstaking. Almost the entire surface of a page-size wooden block had to be carved away, leaving a few raised areas that would print on the page. Once a block was carved, it could be used to print only one page of text, although it could be used to print hundreds of copies of that same page. To produce a one-hundred-page book, printers had to carve one hundred separate blocks. This took a great deal of time. In 932, a group of Confucian printers began to block print

a complete, 130-volume edition of Confucius's teachings. It took twenty-one years for the printers to complete their work.

Movable Type

Chinese printers soon began to search for ways to print books more quickly. One such printer was named Pi Sheng. He thought of cutting the large printing block into many smaller blocks with one word on each. The smaller blocks, known as type, could be fitted together like pieces of a mosaic to print a complete page of text. The type could then be taken apart and rearranged to form a new page. This invention came to be known as movable type. It saved printers from having to carve a new printing block for every page they wanted to print.

Pi Sheng knew wooden type would chip, splinter, and wear out easily. If he wanted to use his type over and over, he needed to make it out of something more durable than wood. Pi Sheng's solution was described by a historian of the Sung Dynasty:

> During the period Ch'ing-li [1041-1048] Pi Sheng, a man of the common people, invented movable type. His method was as follows: He took sticky clay and cut it in characters as thin as the edge of a copper coin. Each character formed . . . a single [piece of] type. He baked them in the fire to make them hard.

Once he had created hard, durable type, Pi Sheng had another problem to solve. He had to figure out how to hold the type together so it would not move during printing. The Sung Dynasty historian reported this solution as well:

FROM BLOCK PRINTING TO MOVABLE TYPE

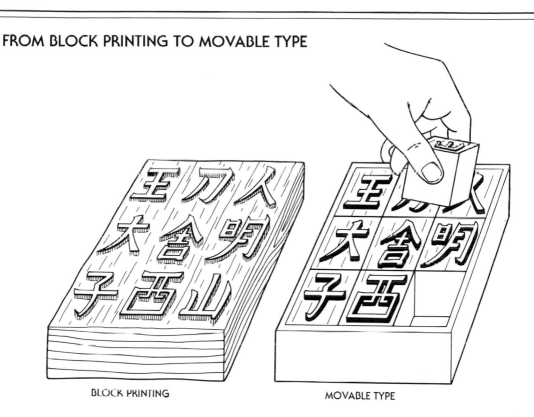

BLOCK PRINTING

MOVABLE TYPE

The earliest form of printing was block printing. It was developed by the Chinese around 750 A.D. Block printing is a slow process because a wooden block must be carved for every original page.

About 1040 A.D., the Chinese printer Pi Sheng invented movable type. This form of printing uses individual pieces of type for each written symbol. These pieces of type can be arranged within a metal frame, then rearranged and used again and again. With movable type, there is no need to carve a new block for each page. Instead, the pieces of type just need to be reset.

He had previously prepared an iron plate and he had covered this plate with a mixture of pine resin, wax, and paper ashes. When he wished to print, he took an iron frame and set it on the iron plate. In this he placed the type, set close together. When the frame was full, the whole made one solid block of type. He then placed it near the fire to warm it. When the paste was slightly melted, he took a smooth board and pressed it over the surface, so the block of type became . . . even.

When the paste cooled, it hardened, holding the type securely in place. Using this method, Pi Sheng was able to print "thousands of copies . . . divinely quick," according to the ancient historian.

Another problem that Pi Sheng and other Chinese printers faced was not so easily solved. It involved the nature of the Chinese language. Instead of using an alphabet to create sounds that can be strung together to make words, the Chinese used separate symbols, known

Chinese typesetters select type from shallow, wooden trays in this eighteenth-century depiction of a typical Chinese print shop. The trays held thousands of separate pieces of type.

In the fourteenth century, Korean printers began experimenting with movable type made of metal. The reason was simple: Korea lacked the hardwoods needed for block printing. Korean forests consisted mostly of pine, a wood too soft to be carved with great precision. The land was rich in metals, however.

The Koreans had become experts at heating these metals until they melted, then pouring the molten metal into molds of different shapes. As the metal cooled, it hardened into the shape of the mold. This process of melting and reshaping metal is known as casting. Korean metalworkers used this process to cast coins. Using the same process, Korean printers cast the world's first metal type. In 1392, the Korean government established a type foundry, a place where metalworkers did casting, because "the king thought with sadness that so few books could be printed without one."

An Alphabet for Printing

Like the Chinese, the Koreans faced a problem of storing and retrieving a large number of type characters. This is because, centuries before, the Koreans had adopted the Chinese system of writing. Realizing the limitations of printing with ideographic symbols, the ruler of Korea, King Sejong the Great (1419–1450), ordered scholars in his court to develop an alphabet expressly for printing books. In 1446, the scholars presented the king with a new, twenty-five-letter alphabet.

The new alphabet worked beautifully with movable type. The government began publishing well-known

as ideograms, for each word in the language. To print with movable type, Chinese printers needed a different piece of type for each word in the language. This amounted to thousands of separate pieces of type. Storing and retrieving this much type presented a great challenge. Some printers kept their type in shallow wooden trays. Others built large wooden wheels divided into many compartments. The type composer could then turn the wheel, like a lazy susan, to bring the desired character within reach. Still, the system was slow and awkward.

By the eighth century, the art of block printing had also spread to Korea.

texts in the new "script for the people," as the king called it. But the king's alphabet did not catch on. Those who might have benefited most from low-cost books, the common people, did not know how to read and had no way to learn. For them, the new books were useless. And the scholars who did know how to read, did not see why they should learn a new alphabet. After all, they had already read nearly all of the books the king ordered to be redone.

Some Korean scholars also preferred the old system for the making of books. With the ideographic system, scholars were able to engrave printing blocks themselves. With the alphabetic system, they had to depend on a variety of artisans to carry out the work for them.

Some Korean printers also preferred block printing. Once a block was carved, it could be used over and over to print an additional copy of a page whenever one was needed. Once a page was printed with movable type, the separate pieces of type used to print it were broken apart and rearranged to print another page. To print an extra copy, all the type used had to be gathered and rearranged to print the page again. The process of arranging movable type on a page is known as typesetting, and it takes a great deal of time.

When Sejong the Great died in 1450, the alphabet and printing methods he encouraged died with him. His people would not print books with movable metal type again for hundreds of years. When they did, it would not be because of Sejong's efforts. Rather, it would be the result of work undertaken by a man who lived halfway around the world, in a distant land called Germany.

That man was Johannes Gutenberg.

Gutenberg's World

Around 1450, the first works printed in Europe with movable type appeared in Mainz, Germany. The oldest surviving fragment comes from a poem entitled "World Judgment" published around 1445. An astronomical calendar and two church documents known as Indulgences seem to have been printed next.

Each of these works appears to have been produced in the same workshop. All were printed with similar type, ink, and paper. None of the specimens bears the name of its printer or the date of the printing, but all four are believed to be the work of a goldsmith, gem polisher, and inventor named Johannes Gutenberg.

Gutenberg's World

Born about 1397, Johannes Gutenberg lived in a world very different from our own. Besides lacking the modern conveniences made possible by the discovery of electricity, Gutenberg also had to do without the ease of travel and communication we enjoy today.

As a result, Gutenberg's world was a small one. He lived his entire life in two German cities, Mainz and Strasbourg, located scarcely one hundred miles apart. He had no newspapers or magazines to read because none existed. The news of his day was spread by word of mouth, by travelers, and storytellers. The people of Mainz gathered at inns and taverns to hear travelers describe what was happening in other cities and in other parts of the world.

Gutenberg himself could read and write, but most people throughout Europe were illiterate. Education was a luxury that only wealthy families could afford. Gutenberg's family was one of these.

Gutenberg's father belonged to the patrician, or land-owning, class. In fact, as a young man, Johannes added the name of the family estate, Gutenberg, to his family name, Gensfleisch. Eventually, he dropped the family name, which means "gooseflesh" in German, and used the estate name, which means

Johannes Gutenberg, inventor of the printing press, lived in a world where news was spread by word of mouth and people gathered at inns and taverns to hear tales from other cities.

Gutenberg most likely learned about metallurgy while working at the mint. His skill in casting, stamping, and engraving proved invaluable when he began to experiment with the casting and cutting of movable type.

only the religious lives of its members but their social and political lives as well.

As much as medieval life differed from life today, it was similar in some ways. Each city had its own government, complete with courts of law. Gutenberg's father was a member of Mainz's city council. Gutenberg himself spent a great deal of time in court, fighting various lawsuits that were brought against him. Much of what we know about Gutenberg's development of the printing press comes from records of these hearings.

As in most societies today, in medieval Europe, goods and services were provided by artisans, craftspeople, and professionals who were paid for their work. Many of the craftspeople belonged to professional associations, known as guilds. The guilds carefully regulated the training, workmanship, and wages of the workers, much as labor unions do today. Carpenters, bakers, blacksmiths, goldsmiths, shoemakers, and other artisans all belonged to separate guilds.

Books of the Middle Ages

Some of the greatest achievements of the Middle Ages occurred in a field of great importance to Gutenberg: the production of books. As he planned the design of his printing press, Gutenberg was greatly influenced by the appearance of the books created during the Middle Ages.

Most of the books produced in this period in Europe were Christian scriptures and religious texts. These works were copied by hand by monks who worked in scriptoria, the writing rooms of Christian monasteries. Because they were handwritten, these books are known as manuscripts, derived from the

"good mountain"—a reasonable choice for a young man with a strong desire to get ahead in the world.

An important figure in the community, Gutenberg's father helped oversee the mint located in Mainz. Most likely, it was at the mint that Johannes learned about metallurgy, the science of metals. The knowledge he gained about how to cast, stamp, and engrave metal coins proved invaluable when he began to experiment with the casting and cutting of movable type.

Like many institutions in Europe, the mint at which Gutenberg learned his trade was operated by the Catholic church. The church at this time was very powerful. Its leaders ruled not

Latin words *manus,* which means "hand," and *scribere,* which means "to write."

Manuscripts were written on specially prepared animal skins. This material, known as vellum or parchment, is ideal for making book pages. Vellum is exceptionally durable, flexible, and opaque. But it is also expensive. The skin of one goat, calf, or sheep yields only two sheets, known as folios. Each folio can be folded once and trimmed to form two leaves, or four pages. At this rate, one hundred calfskins were needed to produce a single eight-hundred page manuscript!

Not all medieval manuscripts were written on vellum, however. Beginning in the eleventh century, some monasteries began to use paper in the production of books. The knowledge of papermaking had spread to Europe through the Arab world. In the eighth century, Arab soldiers conquered portions of western China and forced their prisoners to teach them how to make paper. This knowledge slowly spread throughout the Arab world, which included part of Spain. In the eleventh century, the first European paper mill was built in Jativa, Spain. By the fifteenth century, paper mills were operating in nearly every country in Europe.

In many scriptoria, the monks worked in absolute quiet so that they could concentrate on their work. In other monasteries, one monk would read a text aloud, and the other monks would write it down. With this method, several copies of a text could be made at once, but the accuracy of the copying depended on the copyists' ability to spell correctly.

The monks worked in a scriptorium during the daylight hours only. Candles were not allowed in the scriptorium for fear of fire. The monks knew that a single fire could wipe out not only their life's work but the work of generations. The scriptoria did not have fireplaces for the same reason. During the winter, the copyists in northern Europe labored in the cold.

Illuminated Manuscripts

The monks who worked in scriptoria believed they should make their books as beautiful as possible to please God. They formed each letter, each word, and each page very carefully. Often

This page from a sixteenth-century prayerbook provides an example of the intricate detail found in the illuminated manuscripts done by the monks.

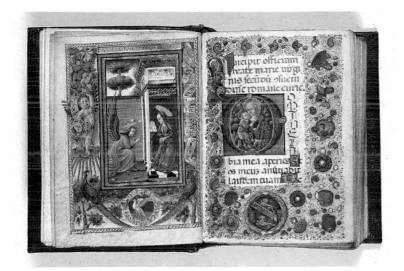

The monks decorated pages with colorful borders, including patterns of vines and flowers, birds, animals, and imaginary beasts, as this Book of Hours from around 1470 shows.

they enlarged the first, or initial, letter of a section of text and decorated it with colored ink. Some monks drew tiny pictures, or miniatures, within the outlines of the initial letters. Eventually, the initial letters of chapters or books were greatly enlarged to accommodate entire scenes.

The monks also decorated the pages with colorful borders. Patterns of

In this thirteenth-century book, the artist uses pen and ink; blue, green, red, and brown washes; gold leaf; and tempera paint. As was common in this period, a tiny picture is drawn within the outlines of the initial letter.

This volume from about 1480 shows the bright colors and intricate borders that characterized many of the manuscripts done by the monks. Crushed lapis lazuli, mercury, sulfur, and gold were used to give rich color to the pages.

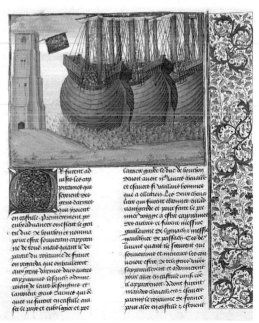

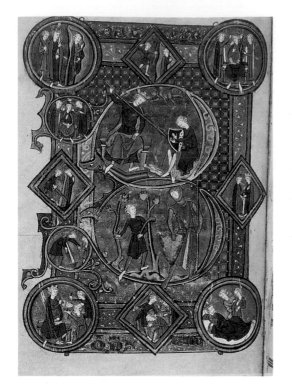

Top left and top right: Books produced in the monasteries, such as this one from the thirteenth century, were prized for their beauty. Wealthy book collectors paid the churches great sums of money to buy illuminated manuscripts.

Bottom left: The artistry of the monks, who believed they should make their books as beautiful as possible to please God, is evident in this scene from the Gospels, done around 1120.

entwined vines and flowers blossomed around the text. Birds, animals, and imaginary beasts peered out from the foliage. Each tiny image was painted in exquisite detail.

The monks also added paintings to illustrate the text. Sometimes, several artists worked together to illustrate one book. Each artist tried hard to match the styles of the others so that the book appeared consistent from page to page.

The monks used bright colors in the paintings, borders, and initial letters of their manuscripts. Some of the paints they used were made of valuable materials. Ultramarine blue was made with crushed lapis lazuli, a semiprecious bright blue stone. Vermillion, a bright red color, included mercury and sulfur. The monks also highlighted many scenes with gold, which was applied to the page in thin sheets known as gold leaf.

Because of the decorations within them, these books became known as illuminated manuscripts. The word *illuminate* is derived from the Latin word *illuminare,* which means "to adorn." At the root of *illuminare* is another Latin word, *luminare,* which means "to light." With their brightly colored pages, the illuminated manuscripts of the Middle Ages deserved their name in the fullest sense.

This picture from The Book of Kells *shows the intricate lettering and painstaking artwork of this unique piece.*

The *Lindisfarne Gospels*

One of the most beautiful illuminated manuscripts in the *Lindisfarne Gospels,* which was produced around A.D. 700 on Lindisfarne, a small island off the coast of northern England. A note made in the book two hundred years after it was completed describes both the work that went into the making of illuminated manuscripts and the attitudes of those who produced them:

> Eadfrith, Bishop of the church of Lindisfarne, he at the first wrote this book for God and for St. Cuthbert and for the whole company of the saints whose relics are on the island. And Ethilwald, Bishop of those of Lindisfarne island, bound and covered it outwardly as well as he could. And Billfrith, the anchorite, he wrought, as a smith, the ornaments that are on the

The Lindisfarne Gospels *is a masterpiece of illumination. This photo taken from one of its pages, shows the book's intricate detail.*

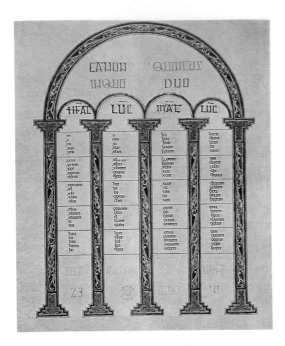

The Lindisfarne Gospels *is filled with complicated patterns and designs.*

outside and adorned it with gold and with gems and gilded silver, unalloyed metal.

The *Lindisfarne Gospels* is a beautiful example of Celtic artistry. Rich in color, it is filled with complicated patterns and ornamental designs. Entire words are formed with letters made of animals, serpents, and birds.

About a century later, another masterpiece of Celtic book design, the *Book of Kells,* was completed at the Abbey of Kells, about forty miles outside of Dublin, Ireland. Like the *Lindisfarne Gospels,* the *Book of Kells* consists of richly decorated texts of the four Gospels. All but two of its pages are illuminated. Even more than the *Lindisfarne Gospels,* the *Book of Kells* swarms with complex designs and detailed illumination. Irish tradition says that for years the book was believed to be the work of angels.

Lay Artisans

The books produced in the monasteries were prized for their beauty by the royalty and nobility of the Middle Ages. Wealthy book collectors paid the churches great sums of money to purchase illuminated manuscripts. To satisfy the demand for these books, the monasteries hired artisans from outside the church and trained them in the art of book production.

These people, known as lay artisans, often specialized in the work they did. Like other craftspeople, the artisans who produced books formed guilds. The production of an illuminated manuscript was divided among four guilds: the parchment makers, the scribes, the illuminators, and the bookbinders.

This page from a medieval Bible includes an elaborate, illuminated initial.

Education in the Middle Ages

Just as the production of books had spread beyond the walls of the church by the time Gutenberg was born, so too had learning and literacy. In the twelfth century, a band of wandering scholars settled in Oxford, England, and formed what was to become Oxford University. Other universities soon followed in Cambridge, Saint Andrews, Glasgow, Dublin, Paris, Avignon, Bologna, Florence, Prague, and other major cities of Europe. Then, as now, doctors, lawyers, schoolmasters, and scholars were expected to study at the university before practicing their profession.

A growing number of children were being educated as well. Children in the countryside attended grade schools founded by monasteries. In cities, many children also attended grade schools run by the church, but some children attended schools provided by hospitals or guilds. Most of the instructors were priests, but by Gutenberg's day, a growing number of teachers came from outside the church. These instructors were known as lay teachers.

Students in elementary schools learned reading, writing, arithmetic, and music. They also studied religious subjects and learn their catechism, the creed, and prayers. Students in secondary schools continued their religious training, but they also learned to read and write Latin, the language of the ancient Romans.

The Language of Learning

It was important for serious students to learn Latin because almost all books were written in Latin. Ever since the

This page from a 1452 Bible is written in Latin, as were all writings of the time.

Romans had conquered Europe in the first century, books had been written in Latin.

Although nearly all of Europe adopted Latin as its spoken language, each country had altered it. Bit by bit, spoken Latin evolved into several new languages: Italian, French, Spanish, and Portuguese. Despite these changes, pure Latin remained the official written language of the Roman Empire, used by scholars and government officials all across Europe.

After the fall of the Roman Empire, in the fifth century, Latin survived as a written language because it was the official language of the Catholic church, just as it is today. As Christianity spread across Europe, Latin spread with it. The books produced by Christian monasteries in the Middle Ages were written in Latin. Since many universities were operated by the church, nearly all scholarly papers were written in Latin. Centuries after it ceased to be an everyday language, Latin remained the language of learning.

The Business of Publishing

Those who could read Latin often wanted books of their own. Some of the guilds that produced manuscripts for the monasteries also began to produce books for scholars, students, and professionals. By the thirteenth century, the majority of European books were produced by commercial workshops rather than by monasteries.

By Gutenberg's day, the business of copying books was a large one. In

Bibles, like this one from the mid-thirteenth century, were not the only books written in Latin. Scholarly papers also were written in Latin because many universities were owned by the Church.

Attention to detail and careful rendering of facial features were characteristic of work done around 1500, as seen in this page from the Book of Hours.

Florence, Italy, a bookseller named Vespansio da Bisticci employed fifty scribes full-time to produce two hundred manuscripts in twenty-two months for Cosimo de' Medici.

The growing trade in books caught Gutenberg's attention. He saw that a bookseller probably could sell as many manuscripts as he could produce. But he also saw that the production of books was slow and costly. It took a single copyist five full months to complete just one manuscript! If only there were a way to speed up the production of books. . . .

There was. Pi Sheng had discovered it four hundred years before. Now it was Gutenberg's turn to do the same.

■■■■■■■■■■ CHAPTER **3**

Gutenberg's Press

Around 1430, Gutenberg moved from Mainz to Strasbourg, where he entered into a partnership with three other men. At first, the partners made mirrors and trinkets. In 1438, they drew up a contract to form a new business. According to the contract, the purpose of the partnership was to exploit "new ideas." The agreement stated that each partner had to pay Gutenberg a sum of money. In return, Gutenberg promised to teach his partners "certain arts and undertakings." All evidence suggests that these arts and undertakings had to do with printing.

It is not clear how much Gutenberg knew about printing before he formed this partnership. The contract suggests that he had already discovered something that the three other men were willing to pay to learn. Court records indicate that within a year the partners had built a type of printing press that used movable type. Either Gutenberg worked very fast, or he had been experimenting with printing before the partnership was formed.

Almost certainly, Gutenberg did not know about the printing done with movable type in the court of Sejong the Great in Korea. He probably had not heard of Chinese experiments with movable type, either. Although the great Italian traveler, Marco Polo, had written a book about his journey to China around 1300, he had said nothing about the books printed with Pi Sheng's movable type.

For many years, some historians believed that Gutenberg learned about movable type from another European. According to a Dutch account written in 1568, Laurens Janzoon Coster carved pieces of movable type from wood and set up the first printing press. In this story, one of Coster's helpers stole the press and ran away to Germany with it. In other words, Gutenberg stole the idea for the printing press from Coster. Few scholars believe this story today. Some historians suggest that a few typeset fragments found in other European cities may predate Gutenberg's work, but these claims remain unproven.

Although Gutenberg probably had not heard of movable type, he certainly

The great Italian explorer, Marco Polo, wrote a book about his journey to China around 1300.

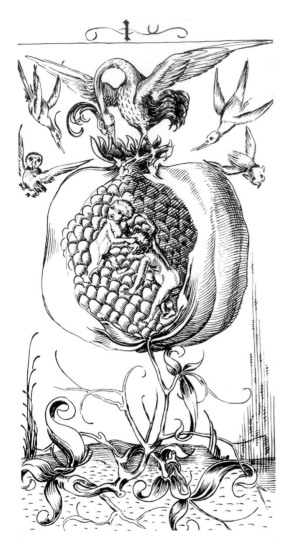

Playing cards, like this one from the fifteenth century in Italy, were among the first items block printed in Europe.

the process used to print them and the paper on which they were printed, playing cards originated in China. By 1404, they had become so popular in Europe that leaders of the Catholic church forbade clergy members to play cards. Around 1440, a beautiful set of playing cards was printed by a person known only as the Master of Playing Cards. Some historians have suggested that the Master of Playing Cards may have been Gutenberg himself.

Whether or not he printed playing cards, Gutenberg knew of them. He had also seen the block-printed pictures, known as woodcuts, that had begun to appear in Europe around 1400. By the time Gutenberg began to work on his press, entire books were being block-printed.

Gutenberg was not interested in block printing, however. It took longer to carve a single printing block than it did to copy many pages by hand. Gutenberg wanted to print an entire book not with many different blocks but with one block that could be changed many times. In other words, he wanted to create a printing block out of many smaller pieces of type, just as Pi Sheng had done.

Gutenberg's task, however, was more difficult than Pi Sheng's. Pi Sheng needed to make a separate piece of type for every word on the page. Gutenberg had to make a separate piece of type for every letter in every word. For example, this sentence consists of only 19 words, but it contains 122 separate letters, spaces, and punctuation marks.

Gutenberg faced another problem. To compete with the fine manuscripts of his day, his pages needed to be not only readable but beautiful. Duplicate letters needed to be uniform in size

knew about another form of Chinese printing: block printing. Upon his return to Europe, Marco Polo had described with amazement how the Chinese paid for things with paper money printed with wooden blocks. After hearing these reports, many Europeans began to experiment with block printing themselves.

Among the first things block printed in Europe were playing cards. Like

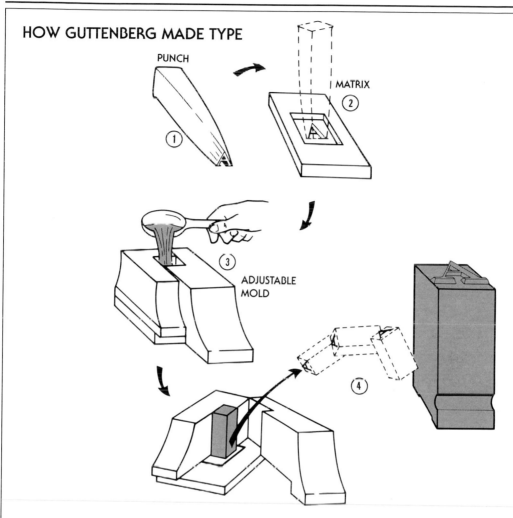

HOW GUTTENBERG MADE TYPE

PUNCH

MATRIX

ADJUSTABLE MOLD

To make, or cast, his type, Gutenberg first made a model of each letter of the alphabet by cutting it in relief on a steel bar, called a punch (1). Then he used the punch to stamp a sunken impression of the letter into a brass square, called a matrix (2). The matrix slid into the bottom of an adjustable mold, and then the mold was filled with molten lead (3). When the lead cooled, the hinged mold was opened and the finished piece of type removed (4).

and shape. Each line of type needed to be straight and parallel to the rest. All of the lines had to measure exactly the same width across the page, length, or be justified, and all of the type had to print with uniform darkness.

Breakthrough

Gutenberg solved all of these problems with one brilliant idea. Like many great discoveries, Gutenberg's breakthrough was very simple. He decided to cast all of his type from a single mold. That way, all of his type would be nearly identical in size. Set in lines, identical type would make uniform rows. Stood on end, it would leave a uniform impression when paper was pressed against it.

The shape Gutenberg came up with for his type was different from the shape used by Pi Sheng or by the printers of Sejong's court. The type created by the Asian printers was flat and round. The type cast by Gutenberg was tall, narrow, and square. An extra metal backing made Gutenberg's type easy to grip with the fingers, and easy to hold with a clamp. The square design meant that when pieces of Gutenberg's type were placed side by side, they fit firmly together.

Gutenberg developed a special mixture of metal, or an alloy, for casting his type. The main ingredients in Gutenberg's type were tin and lead, metals that are easy to melt. His recipe also included a rare metal called antimony. Unlike most metals, antimony does not shrink when it cools. This was important because even a small amount of shrinkage would have created type that was impossible to fit together tightly. By mixing antimony with lead and tin, Gutenberg ensured that his type would not cool into warped or uneven shapes.

To cast his type, Gutenberg carved a letter out of the end of a metal rod. Since he wanted his printed books to look like the handwritten books of his day, Gutenberg made his letters identical to those drawn by the copyists at the Mainz scriptorium. This lettering style, known as Gothic Script, included many straight lines and square corners. These shapes were easier to cut into metal than sweeping curves would have been.

Using a carved rod, known as a punch, Gutenberg stamped the letter into another piece of metal, known as a matrix. He placed the matrix at the bottom of his type mold, which was shaped like a tall box, and poured molten metal into an opening at the top. The metal trickled down the inside of the box to the indented matrix below. The metal filled the matrix, then filled the box above it. When the metal cooled, it formed a metal shaft with a raised letter on one end. To remove the type from the mold, Gutenberg opened a hinged door on one side of the mold and slid the type out.

To make type for a different letter, Gutenberg simply changed the matrix. He made the sides of the mold adjustable so that he could vary the width of the type a little bit. In this way, Gutenberg was able to cast wide letters like *w* and *m* with the same mold he used for narrow letters like *i* and *t* and medium letters like *o* and *e*. Everything else stayed the same, and each piece of type was nearly identical in width and height.

The Chase

Once he had cast enough type to make up a page, Gutenberg had to find a way to hold the type together so that it would not shift or wobble when paper was pressed against it. Even the slightest movement would create smeared, fuzzy letters.

Pi Sheng had solved this problem by placing his type on an iron plate coated with paste, then surrounding the type with an iron frame. Gutenberg's solution was almost identical. He also placed his type on an iron bed and surrounded it with an adjustable metal frame, known as a chase. Instead of using paste to hold his type in place, however, Gutenberg used pressure. He

Print shop workers squeeze type into an iron bed surrounded by an adjustable metal frame. To keep the type from shifting, they fill the empty spaces with bars and then wedge the type between the bars and the frame.

placed bars inside the frame to fill up the empty spaces, then adjusted the chase until it fit tightly around the bars. Finally, he drove small wedges between the bars and the chase, squeezing the block of type together so that it could not move.

The bars Gutenberg placed inside his chase were very important. He made them slightly shorter than the shafts of type. That way, when paper was pressed down onto the inked block of type, it touched the letters but not the bars. The ink on the letters was transferred onto the paper, but the ink on the bars was not. The bars left blank spaces on the page, known as negative space.

Negative space is very important to the appearance and readability of a page. If words or letters are printed too close together, they are difficult to read. If lines of text are too close together or unevenly spaced, they, too, are difficult to read. If the page is crammed with text, it appears crowded and unattractive.

Gutenberg's system of type and space bars allowed him to control the negative space on his page with great precision. He used narrow bars to cre-

ate neat breaks between words. He placed line-length bars, known as leading, between rows of type to provide space above and below each line of text for easy reading. He inserted wider bars to form margins around the text. Gutenberg cast the different space bars himself, so each kind was uniform in size, making the spaces on his printed page even and attractive.

The Press

Once Gutenberg had invented his type mold and chase, his work on the press was nearly complete. He did not need to invent a device to press the paper against the type. Such a device already existed. All Gutenberg had to do was adapt it to his needs.

For centuries, wine makers had used wooden presses to crush grapes. At the center of the press was a large wooden screw. As it turned through a threaded hole, the screw moved up and down. Attached to the screw was a wooden board, known as a platen. A few inches below the platen was another board, known as the bed. The wine maker heaped grapes onto the bed, then turned the screw. The screw lowered the platen toward the bed, crushing the grapes.

Gutenberg and his partners hired a man named Conrad Saspach to build a similar press for them. They probably had Saspach modify the design of the winepress slightly. The bed of the printing press was shaped so that it would hold a chase. Also, the bed was designed to slide in and out, beneath the platen. A hinged frame was attached to the bed. This frame was designed to hold a sheet of paper or vellum. To load a sheet of paper into the press, Gutenberg swung the frame up. Once the sheet was in place, he lowered the frame over the chase.

Gutenberg and his partners admire the first words ever printed in Europe with movable type.

Gutenberg modeled his printing press after the wooden grape presses used for centuries by wine makers. A large wooden screw attached to a wooden board pressed the paper firmly against an inked bed of type.

To try out his press, Gutenberg smeared ink all over the type with leather-covered balls. He loaded a sheet of paper into the frame, then carefully positioned the frame above the type. He slid the bed of the press under the platen, then grasped the handle attached to the wooden screw. He turned the screw gently, lowering the platen until it touched the back of the frame. Pulling the handle harder, he pressed the paper firmly against the type. Reversing the direction of the screw, he raised the platen, then slid out the bed. As his partners looked on, Gutenberg raised the frame and took a long, admiring look at the first words ever printed in Europe with movable type.

Disaster Strikes

No sooner had Gutenberg succeeded in building a workable press than disaster struck. One of his three partners,

Andrew Dritzehen, died. Dritzehen's brothers asked to take Andrew's place in the partnership, as permitted in the contract. Gutenberg refused, offering instead to refund their brother's money, an option also permitted by the contract. The brothers sued Gutenberg, but the court agreed his offer was fair. Gutenberg won the legal battle, but it cost him precious time and money.

Nothing more is known about what Gutenberg or his partners did until 1442, when Gutenberg borrowed money from the Saint Thomas Parish in Strasbourg. The loan suggests that Gutenberg and his partners needed funds to keep their work going. In 1443, the partners' five-year contract expired. The partnership dissolved without having produced a single work.

Sometime afterward, Gutenberg left Strasbourg and returned to Mainz. There, Gutenberg borrowed more money, this time from Arnold Gelthuss, a relative. It is not known how many printing materials Gutenberg had brought with him from Strasbourg, but presum-ably he brought some. Shortly after signing for the loan from Gelthuss, Gutenberg produced his first works—a poem, a calender, and two Indulgences. How well these works sold remains unclear. Within two years of receiving the loan from Gelthuss, Gutenberg once again sought financial help.

A Costly Decision

This time Gutenberg turned to a prominent lawyer named John Fust. In 1450, Fust loaned Gutenberg eight-hundred guldens, more than four times the amount Gutenberg borrowed from Saint Thomas Parish in Strasbourg. Gutenberg's business must have shown considerable promise at this time; otherwise, Fust would not have loaned the printer such a large sum of money. Perhaps Gutenberg won Fust's confidence by revealing his master plan. He wanted to produce a Bible. The Bible was one of the most popular books of the time, and Gutenberg could reasonably expect to sell as many copies as he could print.

Gutenberg's invention radically changed printing. Here, he pulls a freshly printed sheet from a bed of type.

Two years later, Fust gave Gutenberg another eight-hundred guldens. This money was not a loan but an investment in the business. Fust was to receive part of the profits from everything Gutenberg sold. Once again, Gutenberg had a partner.

Printing a Bible was a huge undertaking. With more than 1,280 pages, each vellum copy would require 160 calfskins. The text on each page would be arranged in two columns of 42 lines each, requiring an average of 2,500 separate pieces of type per page. Altogether, more than 290 separate letters and symbols needed to be cast, including uppercase and lowercase letters, punctuation marks, and hyphens. To speed production, Gutenberg probably used two presses right from the start, eventually adding as many as six. Most likely, Gutenberg cast enough type to make up two full chases of type, or forms, for each press. As a result, he and his assistants could typeset one page while another was being printed. That meant Gutenberg had to cast more than 30,000 separate pieces of type!

One of the assistants Gutenberg hired was Peter Schöffer, the son-in-law of John Fust. An experienced artist, Schöffer had worked in Paris as a scribe and as a manuscript illuminator. Gutenberg made Schöffer the foreman of his print shop. Schöffer began to design colored initials to decorate the printed page, just as the monks decorated their illuminated manuscripts.

Completing a Life's Work

Gutenberg and his shop labored for five long years to print 210 copies of the Bible—30 on vellum and 180 on paper. In 1455, when work on the Bible was nearly complete, Gutenberg was summoned to court. John Fust was suing him for immediate repayment of his loans. After a hearing, the court ordered Gutenberg to repay the original loan and a portion of the second investment, plus interest. The total settlement came to 2,026 guldens, far more than Gutenberg could possibly afford. As a result, the court ordered Gutenberg to give all of his assets—his presses, his type, and his nearly completed Bibles—to Fust.

As soon as he gained control of Gutenberg's print shop, Fust put his son-in-law in charge of the printing operation. A few months later, Fust and Schöffer issued their first Bible. The

Print shops, like this one in 1520 in Germany, sprouted up all over Europe as word of Gutenberg's invention spread.

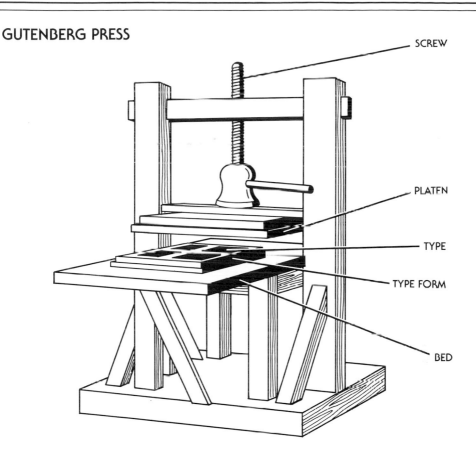

GUTENBERG PRESS

SCREW

PLATEN

TYPE

TYPE FORM

BED

Invented around 1442, Gutenberg's press was a converted wine press. It was quite simple but time-consuming to operate. First, the inked, movable metal type was placed on a flat bed. A sheet of paper was placed over the type. Then a heavy, flat board, called a platen, was pressed firmly down onto the paper by tightening a thick wooden screw. This caused the type to make an impression on the paper. With Gutenberg's press, one could print about ten sheets of paper per hour.

book itself does not include the name of its printer, but ever since its appearance, the book has been known throughout the world—simply and aptly—as the Gutenberg Bible.

A Masterpiece

The Gutenberg Bible is a masterpiece of book design. Its letters are beautifully formed and exceptionally clear. The text and negative space are well-balanced and attractive. The large initials are handsomely drawn and brilliantly colored. The Gutenberg Bible is one of the most beautiful books ever printed. It is also one of the most important.

The appearance of the Gutenberg Bible marked the beginning of a new

The Gutenberg Bible is a masterpiece of book design. One of the few remaining copies is housed in the Library of Congress in Washington, D.C.

age in the history of civilization. Once copies of this book began to circulate throughout Europe, the value of the printing press became clear. "There has been discovered in Germany a wonderful new method for the production of books," wrote Frenchman Guillaume Fichet in 1470, "and those who have mastered the art are taking it from Mainz out into the world. . . . The light of this discovery will spread from Germany to all parts of the world."

Fichet was right. By 1500, more than one thousand other printers had set up shop, using Gutenberg's invention. Hundreds of thousands more would follow in the centuries to come. Because of the printing press, knowledge would spread farther and faster

than ever before, and change would occur more rapidly.

Nearly every person who has lived after Gutenberg has been touched by his invention in some way—through books, magazines, newspapers, pamphlets, and posters they read. Postage stamps, product packaging, and maps would not have been possible without Gutenberg's innovation. Printing is everywhere.

The changes brought about by the printing press have been so great that we call the results a revolution. These changes fall into four major areas: language, education, religion, and politics. Each revolution influenced the others, and they all began at once.

Revolutionary Changes

One of the first things affected by the invention of the printing press was language itself. Before the Gutenberg Bible appeared, the vast majority of European books were written in Latin, the language of learning that survived from Roman times. Only a few books were written in the language of common speech, known as the vernacular. Gradually over a period of two centuries, the situation would be reversed. Most books would be written in the vernacular, and only a few would be written in Latin. The printing press played an important role in the decline of Latin and the rise of the written vernacular.

The Gutenberg Bible itself was written in Latin. Gutenberg chose as his text the Vulgate Bible, translated into Latin from the original Greek and Hebrew by Saint Jerome between A.D. 383 and 405. Gutenberg, Fust, and Schöffer designed their Bible to be a luxury edition, appealing to scholars and wealthy book collectors. They felt this was the surest way to make a profit with the printing press.

Indeed, Fust and Schöffer must have sold quite a number of these Bibles because their shop quickly grew into Europe's largest and most profitable publishing company. With the help of another wealthy citizen of Mainz, Dr. Conrad Humery, Gutenberg founded another print shop and produced another Bible. The columns of text in this Bible were made up of thirty-six lines. This work is known as the

thirty-six-line Bible to distinguish it from the forty-two-line Bible that Gutenberg produced with Fust and Schöffer. Although he completed this and several other books before he died in 1468, Gutenberg never achieved the commercial success enjoyed by Fust and Schöffer.

As soon as Gutenberg's first Bible appeared, dozens of artisans flocked to Mainz to learn the new art of printing. All of these early printers copied Gutenberg's technical methods. Most followed his business plan as well, producing Latin titles for highly educated buyers. But some early printers followed a different plan. These printers immediately began to publish books in the vernacular. They saw that while the majority of copyists still produced fine copies of Latin works, a growing number were producing works written in the vernacular.

Some of the most popular books of Gutenberg's day had been written and produced by scribes in the vernacular, including Chaucer's *Canterbury Tales*, Dante's *Divine Comedy*, and the tales of King Arthur. Vernacular fables and lore about animals, known as bestiaries, were also popular. So were instructions on making medicines from plants, known as herbals. Since books in the vernacular were intended for common people, scribes produced them as quickly as possible to keep the price of the books low. As a result, these books often appeared simple, even crude. To a few early printers, it seemed that

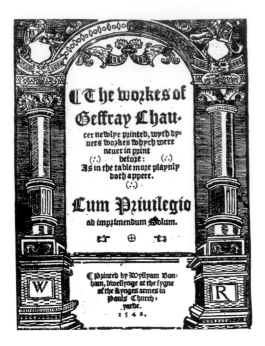

The Canterbury Tales *by Geoffrey Chaucer was one of the most popular books written in the language of common speech known as the vernacular.*

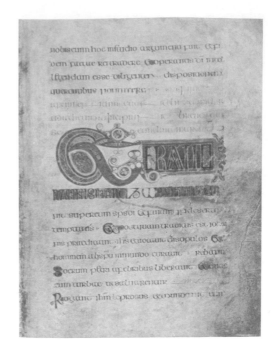

Albrecht Pfister combined two "firsts" in printing with the publication of Edelstein *by Ulrich Boner. Not only was it the first book printed in the Vernacular, it contained colorful woodcuts.*

printing was more naturally suited to imitating the appearance of these books rather than the fine manuscripts written in Latin.

One of these printers was Albrecht Pfister of Germany. In 1461, Pfister was the first European printer to use movable type to publish a book in the vernacular. The book was *Edelstein,* a popular collection of fables written in German by Ulrich Boner in 1349.

Many other printers followed Pfister's example. In 1472, Johann Neumeister of Mainz set up shop in the Italian city of Foligno and published the first printed version of Dante's *Divine Comedy.* In 1474, an Englishman named William Caxton produced the first book printed in English, *Recuyell of the Histories of Troye.* At the time, Caxton lived and worked in the Netherlands, but in 1476

he returned to England and established the first English press. On November 18, 1477, Caxton completed the first book printed on English soil, *Dictes or Sayengis of the Philosophers.* Over the next fifteen years, he published ninety-eight books, seventy-four of which were printed in English. Publishing in the vernacular was becoming more popular.

Many of the best-sellers of the fifteenth century were in the vernacular. One of the most popular was *Narrenschiff,* or *Ship of Fools,* written by Sebastian Brant in 1494. Written in German, it was translated more than a dozen times. Next to the Bible, it is generally considered to be the most widely read book of the time.

As works written in the vernacular became more popular, more and more publishers printed books in the everyday languages of Europe. This began to have a curious effect on the languages themselves.

The Forming of National Languages

When printed books first appeared in the vernacular, the people of Europe spoke a dozen or so major languages. People in the areas that had once been part of the Roman Empire spoke the Romance languages: Italian, French, Spanish, and Portuguese. People outside the old empire spoke the Germanic languages: German, Dutch, English, Welsh, Gaelic, Danish, Swedish, Norwegian, and Icelandic.

In countries where the people lived close together, as in Iceland, everyone spoke the same version of the language. But in larger countries, people in different areas altered their language slightly, creating different versions of the language, called dialects. For exam-

William Caxton produced the first book printed in English in 1474 while living in the Netherlands.

ple, the French spoke at least five different versions, or dialects, of French. In addition, major dialects were further divided into many local dialects. As a result, a person in one town in France might not be able to understand someone from a distant town, even though they both supposedly spoke French.

Caxton reads the first proof-sheet from his new printing press. In fifteen years' time, he published ninety-eight books, seventy-four of which were in English.

When early publishers produced books in the vernacular, they printed these works in the dialects they knew. When people from other towns and regions read these books, they became familiar with the publishers' dialects. Through reading, published dialects spread across each nation, and unpublished dialects died out. In this way, the printing press played a role in standardizing each country's language.

In nearly every European country, the book printed in the vernacular that did the most to standardize each language was the Bible. In France, John Calvin's fifteenth-century translation of the Bible helped standardize French. In England, an edition of the Bible produced by forty-seven translators at the direction of King James I in 1611 shaped the English language for centuries. In Germany, Martin Luther's translation of the Bible, published in 1522, established the New High German of Upper Saxony as Germany's national language.

A Religious Revolution

Luther's translation of the Bible was also significant in other ways. It not only shaped the German language and literature but German thought as well. Its publication played an important role in the Reformation, a religious movement founded and led by Luther.

A priest himself, Luther believed that the Catholic church, centered in Rome, had strayed from its original mission of spreading the message of the Bible. He attacked the church for creating customs and traditions that had no basis in the Christian Scriptures. He urged Christians to base their faith on the wisdom of the Bible, and

Martin Luther's translation of the Bible established the New High German of Upper Saxony as Germany's national language. Luther's translation also played an important role in the Reformation.

he used the printing press to spread this message across Europe.

Luther summarized his beliefs in a document known as the 95 Theses. He pinned this document to the door of a church in Wittenberg in October 1517, openly challenging the leaders of the church in Rome. Local printers immediately copied this document and published it. Within two weeks, copies of the Theses had spread across all of Germany. Within a month, they were known throughout Europe. Thousands of Catholics—priests and average churchgoers alike—rallied behind Luther's proposed reforms. The Reformation had begun.

One of Luther's next steps was to translate the Bible from Latin into German. Knowing that few Catholics understood the ancient Roman language, Luther felt it was important to have a version of the Bible written in everyday speech. He spent several years translat-

Luther looks at a Latin Bible, which he spent several years translating into German.

ing the Scriptures himself. Even if people could not read his translation, they would at least understand it when it was read to them. The publication of Luther's Bible posed another challenge to the Catholic church, which still maintained Latin as its official language.

Luther's Bible, like his teachings, gained an immediate following. During his lifetime, 100,000 copies of his New Testament were published in Wittenberg alone. Dozens of other editions were printed in other German cities, making Luther's Bible the most widely owned book in Germany.

Because of his actions, Luther was not allowed to remain a member of the Catholic church. He continued to preach and write, however, and he and his followers formed a new church. Because this new church was formed out of protest, it became known as the Protestant church, and its members became known as Protestants.

Thanks to the printing press, the Reformation also spread across Europe. Traveling scholars, students, and peddlers carried Luther's books to the Netherlands, France, Italy, Spain, and England. His works outsold everything else in Paris in 1520. In 1521, the German scholar Erasmus wrote, "Luther's books are everywhere and in every language. No one would believe how widely he has moved men." Historian Will Durant put it succinctly, "Printing was the Reformation; Gutenberg made Luther possible."

Luther, pictured here celebrating Christmas with his family, was banished from the Catholic church. He continued to preach and write and eventually he and his followers formed a new church.

A Boost to Education

After the invention of the printing press, the number of schools, libraries, and universities steadily increased. The literacy rate rose to new heights. But to say that Gutenberg's invention caused these things to happen is an exaggeration. All of these trends were well established before Gutenberg was born. No doubt they would have continued with or without his invention. The demands of the changing world required it. Europe was moving from an agricultural society to an industrial one. Commerce was on the rise. Education, once a luxury, was becoming a necessity.

That is not to say that printing had no effect on learning. On the contrary, it affected learning in many ways, large and small.

Authors and educators of the Middle Ages had long been troubled by the fact that copyists made numerous errors in their manuscripts. "Pray I God that none miswrite thee," wrote Chaucer at the end of his poem, *Troilus and Criseyde,* voicing the hopes of authors everywhere. Of course, errors could be made in the typesetting of a book as easily as they could be made in the copying of one. But errors found by the proofreading of a typeset text could be easily corrected before a book was issued. Once a text was corrected, large numbers of accurate copies could be produced at one time. "What was epoch-making in Gutenberg's process," wrote S. H. Steinberg in *Five Hundred Years of Printing,* "was the possibility of editing, sub-editing, and correcting a text which was (at least in theory) identical in every copy."

The fact that copies of printed editions were identical meant that scholars

Aldus Manutius, a Venetian publisher shown in this scene at his printing company, was the first to number book pages. Page numbers made it easy to find important passages in seconds.

exchanging letters could refer to certain pages of books without confusion. In manuscript editions, each book was unique. The same text did not always appear on the same page in every copy of the same book. In printed books, it did.

The advantages printed books offered to scholars increased in 1499 when Aldus Manutius, a Venetian publisher, numbered the pages of a book for the first time. With this handy innovation, important paragraphs and sentences could be found in seconds.

Other book publishers took steps to make books easier to use. William Caxton included a table of contents in the books he produced in 1481. The idea was to let potential buyers know what was in a book so that they would buy it. A table of contents also made it easier for a student or scholar to locate information in a book after buying it. Early in the sixteenth century, publishers began listing a book's topics in alphabetical order along with the page numbers where each topic appeared. These lists, known as indexes, made research easier.

As printed books became easier to use, professionals began to rely on them as a way to store information. Just as today, many of the books printed in the fifteenth and sixteenth centuries were technical in nature. Lawyers, surgeons, apothecaries, and others built up private collections of such manuals to hold the vast number of facts they needed to know for their work but could not possibly remember.

Not all of the effects the printing press had on scholarship were positive, however. For example, before the printing press, scholars in all parts of Europe communicated in Latin. With the coming of the printing press, scholars within each nation began to write and publish in their national language. As a result, scholars in Mainz could no longer understand papers written in Rome or Paris. Students, teachers, and lecturers could no longer travel from city to city secure in the knowledge that Latin would be spoken at every college. Communication between scholars in different countries broke down. Ideas became more isolated.

Within each country, however, printing widened the influence of books. Even people who could not read benefited from printing. As books became more plentiful, those who were literate often read to those who were not. Night after night, in cities, towns, and villages across the countryside, laughter rang out from inns and taverns as the books of Europe's most popular authors were read aloud.

During the day, master craftspeople hired people to read in their shops. Some of these readings were for enter-tainment; others were for instruction. Often technical manuals were read so the workers could learn new skills while they worked.

As books became more common-place, a growing number of common people realized they were capable of writing books. Latin was no longer needed for writing or research. The printing press allowed a whole new class of people to participate in scholarly pursuits. Scarcely more than one hundred years after the invention of the printing press, a glove maker's son named William Shakespeare would write what many consider the greatest plays of the English language.

Words were not the only form of knowledge spread by the printing press. Printers churned out stacks of art and music as well. Through printed art, the great Italian artist Michelangelo studied the work of the German engraver Martin Schongauer. Another Italian artist, Andrea del Sarto, studied the work of the German artist Albrecht Dürer, and Dürer studied the work of an Italian artist named Andrea Mantegna. The invention of music printing in 1500 made it easier for composers to study others' work as well.

Printed Books Versus Manuscripts

Not all people immediately welcomed printed books. In fact, many wealthy book collectors disdained printed books. In 1482, an Italian manuscript dealer named Vespasio da Biticci described the Duke of Urbino's attitude toward printed books this way:

> In this library all the volumes are of perfect beauty, all written by skilled

Encouraged by such words and by the continued demand for their product, most scribes continued practicing their craft. Often, scribes were hired by printers to help make printed books look handwritten. The scribes decorated these books with gold leaf trim, hand-drawn capital letters, just like illuminated manuscripts. Some printers even paid scribes to connect the printed letters to make their books look like manuscripts.

As printed books became more popular, scribes had trouble finding employment. In 1534, scribes in Paris

Some printers hired scribes to give printed books a handwritten look. Pictured here is a page from a fifteenth-century book.

Some people, especially wealthy book collectors, disdained printed books. They preferred books like this Book of Hours from 1524, that had been hand-printed by scribes.

scribes on parchment and many of them adorned with exquisite miniatures. The collection contains no single printed book. The Duke would be ashamed to have a printed book in his library.

An abbot writing a few years later displayed a similar attitude:

A work written on parchment could be preserved for a thousand years, while it is probable that no volume printed on paper will last for more than two centuries. . . . The scribe who ceases his work because of the printing press can be no true lover of books. . . . The printer has no care for the beauty and the artistic form of his books, while with the scribe this is a labor of love.

Print shops, like the one depicted in this illustration from 1568, alarmed those who held power. They feared the printing press might promote beliefs and attitudes that would challenge authority.

and tearing one another's eyes out to get hold of them."

The surge of interest in books and learning sent shock waves through European society. Those who held power were alarmed by the sudden spread of learning and ideas. They feared that the printing press might promote beliefs and attitudes that would challenge their authority.

They were right.

banded together to ask King Francis I to outlaw the printing press. The French ruler agreed to do it, but the law was never enforced. By then, printed books were being purchased by scholars, students, professionals, and artisans. They were included in some of the finest libraries in the world, including those of the Medici family in Florence, King Ferdinand in Naples, and the pope in Rome. The printing press was too popular to be stopped.

"At this very moment a whole wagon load of classics, of the best Aldine editions, has arrived from Venice," wrote one scholar to another in a sixteenth-century letter. "Do you want any? If you do, tell me at once, and send the money, for no sooner is such a freight landed than thirty buyers rise up for each volume, merely asking the price,

Freedom of the Press

Some of the changes brought about by the invention of the printing press were immediate and obvious. The sheer number of published books rose dramatically. When Gutenberg began work on his press, fewer than one million books existed in Europe. By 1500, that number had grown to ten million. Before the end of the fifteenth century, Venetian scribes reported that their city was "stuffed with books."

Other changes, like the decline of Latin, occurred more slowly and went largely unnoticed at first. One of the slowest but most important changes brought about by the invention of the printing press was in the area of politics.

When Gutenberg invented the printing press, the people of Europe were ruled by kings and queens. These leaders inherited their power through their families. But Europeans who read the works of Greek and Roman writers published by Aldus Manutius and others soon found that other forms of government had existed before the European monarchies. Both the Greeks and the Romans had practiced forms of self-rule known as democracy. Under this system, leaders were elected to positions of authority, not born into them.

People who read found that many people—not just the members of royalty—possessed wisdom. They wondered why wise people were not allowed to take part in the ruling of their nations. Here and there, a few brave people put such thoughts into writing. A few even braver people dared to print them.

"If possible, there should be a check on the printing presses," the German scholar Erasmus wrote to the pope in 1523. Erasmus was worried about the challenge Martin Luther posed to the Catholic church, but his advice would be echoed by political leaders for centuries afterward. Widespread knowledge led to questioning of the social order, and nothing spread knowledge as quickly as the printing press.

Newsbooks

Among the first people to recognize that the printing press could shape political thinking were the kings and queens themselves. They knew that good news about their actions strengthened their ability to govern, while bad news weakened it. During a war, for example, news of a successful battle could help a king gather together a larger army. News of a defeat could make raising that army nearly impossible.

One of the first European monarchs to use the printing press to influence public opinion was Henry VII of England. In 1486, Henry received a document from Rome that expressed the pope's support for his claim to the English throne. Henry ordered that hundreds of copies of the document be printed and sent throughout the kingdom to persuade all doubters that he was the new, rightful king.

Henry VII of England, pictured here, was one of the first European monarchs to use the printing press to influence public opinion.

The most important newsbook of the fifteenth century detailed the successful voyage to the new world of explorer Christopher Columbus.

Documents printed for such purposes were known as relations, or newsbooks. Unlike a newspaper, a newsbook reported on only one event. Most were pamphlets, measuring about 5.5 inches wide and 8.5 inches tall and containing from four to twenty-eight pages. Like books of the time, many newsbooks often contained large initial letters and woodcuts.

Probably the most important newsbook of the fifteenth century came from the court of King Ferdinand and Queen Isabella of Spain. Published in April of 1493, it detailed the successful voyage of an Italian adventurer who had sailed westward under the Spanish flag in 1492. That man was Christopher Columbus.

"I have found a great many islands peopled with inhabitants beyond number," Columbus reported in a personal letter that Ferdinand and Isabella immediately ordered to be published. "The mountains and hills, and plains and fields, and land . . . [are] beautiful and rich for planting and sowing, for breeding cattle of all sorts, for building of towns and villages. There could be no believing, without seeing, such harbors as are here, as well as the many and great rivers and excellent waters, most of which contain gold."

The printing press carried news of Columbus's discovery to every corner of Europe. Three separate editions of Columbus's letter were printed in Barcelona in April. A Latin translation of the letter also appeared in Rome within the month. Two more editions appeared in Rome that year, three in Paris, and one each in Antwerp, Belgium; Basel, Switzerland; and Florence, Italy.

News Ballads

Some of the most popular newsbooks were written in poetic form. These newsbooks, known as news ballads, were usually printed on a single-sided sheet of paper known as a broadside. Often read aloud or sung to people who could not read, these reports were many times set to the rhythms of popular songs. Less than three months after it was first published, Columbus's letter was turned into a news ballad by Giuliano Dati, a Florentine poet, who translated the account into the Tuscan language.

Censorship

Ferdinand and Isabella understood the power of the printing press to spread the good news about Columbus's voyage. Realizing what the press could do, the Spanish rulers began to worry that the press might spread bad news about their court as well. To keep bad reports from circulating, Ferdinand and Isabella declared in 1502 that Spanish printers had to obtain permission from the government before printing anything. If the government authorities thought a news story would hurt the monarchy, they would not allow it to be printed. This kind of restriction is known as censorship.

Leaders of other European nations soon followed the Spanish example. In 1521, the rulers of Germany required printers to obtain government permission before printing any work. The censors stopped the publication of anything that criticized the government. The English monarchy issued a similar decree in 1538. In England, censorship was enforced by the printers themselves. The printers formed an organi-

King Ferdinand and Queen Isabella of Spain, who appear here, realized that the printing press could be used to spread bad news as well as good news.

zation called the Stationers Company to register all printed works. Members of the Stationers Company routinely searched all print shops and warehouses for publications that criticized the monarchy.

Sedition Laws

In 1561, the leaders of France also outlawed the printing of material that criticized the government. Printers who violated this decree committed a crime known as sedition, which is inciting people to resist their authorities. Those convicted of sedition for the first time were whipped. Those found guilty a second time were hanged. Between 1600 and 1756, more than eight hundred French writers, publishers, and booksellers were imprisoned or executed for sedition.

Because the penalties for sedition were severe, most printers avoided criticizing the monarchies. Instead, they reported good news about the monarchies, and published accounts of crimes (especially murders), miracles, wonders, unusual births, strange beasts, witchcraft, diseases, floods, fires, the weather, and sports. One newsbook was devoted to "Tidings of a Huge and Ugly Child Born at Arnheim in Gelderland." Another was entitled "A True Relation of the Birth of Three Monsters in the City of Namen in Flaunders." The stories in today's tabloid newspapers resemble those of sixteenth-century newsbooks.

With their sedition laws in place, most sixteenth-century monarchs believed that the printing press was strengthening their rule. But they were wrong. The press was weakening the monarchies, even as it reported their triumphs. For example, in 1571, Queen Elizabeth of England had the Duke of Norfolk arrested and held in the Tower of London for plotting to remove her from the throne and to replace her with the Catholic ruler of Scotland, Mary Queen of Scots. The Duke of Norfolk wanted to reestablish a Catholic monarchy by overthrowing Elizabeth, a Protestant. Once Elizabeth had the Duke arrested, she ordered a newsbook prepared that explained why "the Duke of Norfolk is newly committed to the tower." It did not matter that the newsbook told only the queen's side of the story. Once common people knew about the queen's action, they discussed it. Most people supported the queen, but those loyal to the Duke of Norfolk felt the queen acted unjustly. Those who wanted Mary to rule also were angered by the action. Opinions were shared. Debate grew. Through incidents like this, common people formed their own ideas about government policies. They began to regard themselves as an important part of society, and they wanted a voice in its affairs. These feelings increased when the news began to be printed on a regular basis.

The First Newspapers

The first printed newspapers appeared in Germany around 1609. These publications looked exactly like newsbooks, but they were different in three important ways. First, they appeared regularly. Second, they covered many different events, not just one. Third, they were consistent in format or name from one issue to the next.

The earliest known newspapers were published by Johann Carolus in Strasbourg and Lucas Schulte in Wolfenbuttel. Both publications first appeared in January 1609. Fifty-two editions of the Strasbourg newspaper appeared weekly in 1609, each carefully numbered and dated. Both newspapers contained brief reports from various cities around Europe, including Prague, Vienna, Venice, and Rome.

Printers all across Europe began to copy Carolus's and Schulte's work. By 1621, weekly newspapers were being printed in Basel, Vienna, Frankfurt, Hamburg, Berlin, Antwerp, Amsterdam, and London. The first newspaper

The first printed newspapers appeared in Germany in 1609. Unlike newsbooks, newspapers appeared regularly, covered many different events, and had a consistent format from one issue to the next.

printed in France appeared in 1631, the first in Italy in 1639, and the first in Spain in 1641.

Rebellion

The rulers of Europe controlled the newspapers as tightly as they controlled the newsbooks, but gradually they lost this power. One of the first places this happened was England.

In 1641, a man named Samuel Pecke began to publish a weekly newspaper entitled *The Heads of Several Proceedings In This Present Parliament.* Even though King Charles had decreed that no one could print news about him or his government, Pecke reported how members of Parliament, led by Oliver Cromwell, were pressing the king for a greater share of power. Because Cromwell's

movement had widespread support, Charles did not have the power to stop the publication of Pecke's newspaper. Within weeks, five more newspapers were also printing news about Parliament and the king.

In 1642, civil war broke out in England. The newspapers that had reported on the tensions between King Charles and Parliament soon began to report on the war between them. For

An English newspaper reported in 1641 how members of Parliament, led by Oliver Cromwell, had pressed the king for a greater share of power.

Newspapers that had reported on tensions between King Charles I, pictured here, and Parliament also reported on the civil war that broke out in England in 1642.

The Press in the American Colonies

The first American newspaper was published by a man who had once been jailed for violating English sedition laws. His name was Benjamin Harris. In 1686, Harris had fled to the American colonies. Four years later, he founded a new newspaper entitled *Publick Occurrences Both FORREIGN and DOMESTICK.*

The first issue of Harris's paper appeared in Boston on September 25, 1690. It told how the Indians of Plymouth had "appointed a day of Thanksgiving to God for . . . His giving them now a prospect of a very Comfortable Harvest." Besides reporting the Thanksgiving, Harris also published a number of stories that disturbed the governor of Massachusetts. The governor immediately banned the sale of the pamphlet. The first issue of *Publick Occurrences* was also the last.

Fourteen years passed before anyone else tried to publish a newspaper in the colonies. The next person who did was John Campbell, also of Boston. By the time Campbell founded the *Boston News-Letter* in 1704, the law that had limited the English press, known as the Licensing Act, had expired. Even so, Campbell took care that his *Boston News-Letter* did not offend the governor or anyone else. He copied much of his news from the newspapers that arrived from England, then added local news from the Boston area. The formula worked. The government allowed the publication of the *News Letter* to continue.

Other colonists, including Benjamin and James Franklin, followed Campbell's example. Newspapers appeared in all major colonial cities, including

the seven years that the civil war lasted, neither the king nor Cromwell had the power to stop English printers from publishing anything they wanted. Freedom of the press was born.

Cromwell's forces defeated the king's army. On January 30, 1649, Charles I was beheaded. Cromwell formed a new government, known as the Commonwealth, and named himself Lord Protector of England. Although Cromwell had once supported a free press, he immediately took steps to censor the newspapers. Once again, printers were required to be licensed, and disloyal editors were jailed. But the dream of a free press did not die. Instead, it spread to another area under British control—the colonies of North America.

The first American newspaper was published in 1690. Benjamin Franklin, pictured here, and other colonists later printed their own newspapers.

Philadelphia, Hartford, Providence, New York, and Baltimore. Gradually, the publishers of these newspapers began to include more stories about politics. Some even criticized the colonial government.

One of these publishers was John Peter Zenger of the *New York Weekly Journal.* In 1735, Zenger published a series of reports that criticized the governor of New York. Zenger was arrested and tried for sedition. According to English law, it did not matter whether or not Zenger's reports were true, only that he printed them. Amazingly, the colonial jury ignored the wording of the sedition law. The members of the jury sided with Zenger's lawyer, who argued that the real issue of the case was "speaking and writing the truth." The

Paul Revere engraved, printed, and published this scene of a bloody massacre of colonists by British troops in Boston in 1770.

Benjamin Franklin used this press, now housed at the National Museum in Washington, D.C., to print his newspapers. He and others used stories critical of the colonial government in their newspapers.

jury set Zenger free, and publishers throughout the colonies felt freer because of it.

Over the next forty years, the British government imposed a number of new taxes on the American colonists. Each time, the emboldened colonial newspapers published the protests of the colonists. In November 1765, Parliament passed the Stamp Act, which placed a tax on paper. The newspapers protested, and the act was repealed in March 1766. In 1767, the Townshend Acts taxed tea, glass, lead, and paint. Again the newspapers printed a number of protests, and the taxes were repealed on all items except for tea. The colonial newspapers not only reported on the growing rebellion, but were part of it.

The protests continued, not only in the newspapers but also in pamphlets. One pamphleteer, Thomas Paine, questioned both British taxes and also British rule. In a pamphlet entitled *Common Sense*, Paine called for an end to the "fraud" of monarchy. Others picked up Paine's theme. "Shall the island BRITAIN enslave this continent of AMERICA, which is ninety-nine times bigger, and is capable of supporting hundreds of

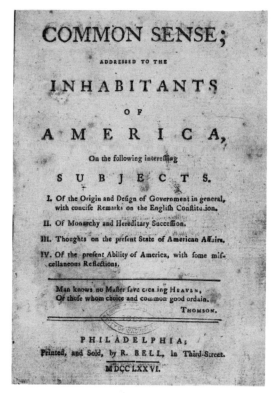

In his pamphlet Common Sense, *Thomas Paine questioned British taxes and called for an end to British rule in the colonies.*

millions of . . . people?" asked the *Massachusetts Spy* in 1773.

After years of public debate, the American colonists declared their inde-

Like other newspapers of the day, the newspaper known as the Massachusetts Spy *or* Thomas's Boston Journal *also took up the cause of freedom from British rule.*

pendence from the British monarchy. The battle turned from one fought with words in the newspapers to one fought with bullets on the battlefield. The revolutionary war lasted eight years. In 1783, the Americans signed a peace treaty, won their freedom, and formed a new government of their own.

One of the leaders of the Revolution, Samuel Adams, believed the true break with Britain occurred "in the hearts and minds of the people" long before the first shot was fired. "The Revolution was effected before the war commenced," Adams wrote. "This radical change in the principles, opinions, sentiments, and affections of the people, was the real American Revolution."

The printing press played a decisive role in "the real American Revolution," according to a writer who called himself "A Countryman." In the March 12, 1766 edition of the *Providence Gazette,* this anonymous person wrote, "Had it not been for the continual informations from the Press, a junction of all the people on this northern continent . . . would have been scarcely conceivable." Another writer, who identified himself as a "Son of Liberty," agreed. Writing in the same issue of the *Providence Gazette,* he declared, "The press hath never done greater service since its first invention."

The First Amendment

Those who formed a new government after the Revolution shared the views expressed in the *Providence Gazette.* In 1789, members of the First Congress drafted an amendment to the Constitution that guaranteed a free press. The First Amendment to the Constitution states, in part, that "Congress shall make no law . . . abridging the freedom of . . . the press."

The portion of the First Amendment that applies to the printing press contains only eleven short words, but millions more have been written about its meaning. It does not mean that printers can publish anything they want. For example, newspapers cannot publish the exact locations of U.S. troops or ships during war. Such reports could lead to many deaths, perhaps even the loss of the war. For similar reasons, newspapers cannot reveal the identities of U.S. spies operating in hostile nations or of undercover law enforcement agents investigating crime.

Congress has passed many laws limiting freedom of the press in special cases like these. When newspaper, magazine, and pamphlet writers and publishers defy such laws, they are arrested, tried, and sometimes convicted for their actions. Some of these convictions have been appealed to the Supreme Court of the United States, where the justices have ruled on the meaning of the First Amendment. In this way, freedom of the press is continually discussed, reviewed, and interpreted.

A Great Experiment

One of the first challenges to the First Amendment came from John Adams, a leader of the American Revolution. Adams, who succeeded George Washington as president, proposed a set of laws known as the Alien and Sedition Acts. These laws were passed by Congress in 1798. Like the sedition laws of the European monarchies, Adams's Sedition Act was written to limit free-

World leaders like Napoleon Bonaparte feared the power of the press. Bonaparte abolished all but four strictly controlled newspapers.

these cases was reviewed by the Supreme Court. Thomas Jefferson, however, defeated Adams for the presidency in 1800 in part because these laws were unpopular. A strong believer in the ability of the common people to rule themselves, Jefferson did not fear a free press. He allowed the Alien and Sedition Act to expire, writing in 1807, that he was conducting "a great experiment" to show that a free press and an orderly government could exist together.

Jefferson's "experiment" with a free press was watched with interest by people around the world, and many chose to copy it. After the French Revolution in 1789, the new government, known as the Constituent Assembly, echoed the U.S. Bill of Rights in its Declaration of the Rights of Man. This document described "the freedom to communicate thoughts and opinions" as "one of the most precious" rights of the French people.

The French experiment with a free press soon ended, however. In 1799, the French leader Napoleon Bonaparte abolished all but four strictly controlled newspapers, stating in a letter, "If I loosened the reins on the press, I would not stay in power three months." A military leader, Napoleon once declared, "Four hostile newspapers are more to be dreaded than a hundred thousand bayonets."

dom of the press. It stated in part: "If any person shall write, print, utter or publish . . . any false, scandalous, or malicious writing . . . against the Government of the United States . . . or the President . . . with intent to defame . . . or to bring them . . . into contempt or disrepute, [that person] shall be punished by a fine not exceeding two thousand dollars, and by imprisonment not exceeding two years."

At least sixteen publishers were arrested for committing seditious libel. Libel is the publication of defamatory, or unfavorable, statements about a person or organization. Among those arrested was Benjamin Franklin's grandson, Benjamin Franklin Bache. None of

A Human Right

Since 1800, many world leaders have adopted Napoleon's view of a free press. These leaders fear that an uncontrolled press could lead to a revolution, as it did in England and the United States. In Germany, where the first

Adolf Hitler was responsible for the burning of thousands of books in Germany.

European books were printed with movable type, the government of Adolf Hitler publicly burned countless books in the 1930s. In China—where paper, ink, and printing all were invented—the present government practices complete censorship of the press. In the last two hundred years, more leaders have abolished freedom of the press than have protected it.

Even so, many of the world's most powerful nations not only allow but cherish a free press. The United States continues to protect the freedom of the press. The nations of Western Europe and Scandinavia have followed the American "experiment," as have nations like Canada, Japan, India, and Israel.

Many of the nations that enjoy a free press have become economic giants. In fact, some people believe a free press encourages business and trade by stimulating a free flow of ideas.

Freedom of the press is now so widely considered a basic human right that a country that does not allow it is considered oppressive. For example, when members of Amnesty International report on human rights around the world, they count a censored press as a measure of oppression. These and other supporters of a free society believe that when a printing press is smashed, it is an act of terrorism. When a book is burned, it is a crime against humanity.

Refinements

The printing methods developed by Johannes Gutenberg did not change very much between 1450 and 1795. For nearly 350 years, printers around the world continued to press sheets of paper against raised metal type just as Gutenberg had. What was printed on the pages changed. The people who read the pages changed. But the basic process of printing them did not.

The changes Gutenberg's followers made were small ones, refinements rather than revolutions. These refinements were made in three basic areas: typography, book illustration, and the press itself.

Type Design

The greatest changes in printing that occurred immediately after the appearance of Gutenberg's press were made in the area of type design. The whole idea of how type should look changed.

Gutenberg designed his type to look like the handwriting of scribes who worked in the Mainz scriptorium. As printed books became widely accepted, printers stopped caring about imitating handwriting. These printers had other concerns. Some wanted to fit more words on each page so they could produce smaller, less expensive books. Others wanted to make books easier to read. Gradually, type began to look less like handwritten letters.

These changes happened because some people found Gutenberg's type difficult to read. Some of the lines in Gutenberg's type were very wide, while others were very narrow, making it hard for the reader to recognize each letter quickly. Gutenberg's closed letters—a, b, d, e, g, o, p, and q—were boxy, containing so little open space that the reader had to strain to recognize each letter. Gutenberg's type also featured spiky points and extra lines that distracted the reader's eye.

Roman Type

Two printers who wanted to change Gutenberg's type were Conrad Sweynheym and Arnold Pannartz. Like most early printers, Sweynheym and Pannartz grew up in Germany and copied Gutenberg's type design. When they set up a print shop in Italy in 1465, they found that the Italians had a hard time reading the ornate German type they brought with them. The Italians were used to reading the handwriting of their own scribes, which was plainer than the German script. To make their books easier for the Italians to read, Sweynheym and Pannartz cast new type modeled after the local lettering style. Because Sweynheym and Pannartz worked near Rome, their type became known as roman type. They produced a number of books in roman type, including *Opera* by Lactantius.

The lines in Sweynheym and Pannartz's letters were all about the same width, unlike those in Gutenberg's type. This made each letter easier to recognize. Sweynheym and Pannartz's closed letters were more circular than Gutenberg's, containing more open space. Readers could see this space at a glance, so they could recognize each letter quickly. Sweynheym and Pannartz also got rid of any extra lines that could confuse the reader.

Perhaps the most important refinement of roman type appeared just four years after Sweynheym and Pannartz introduced it. This change occurred in an edition of Cicero's *Epistolae ad Familiares* published in 1468 by another German printer located in Italy, Johannes da Spira. Da Spira, whose shop was located in Venice, produced a type that had small, horizontal lines at the base of each letter. These lines, known as feet, or serifs, help the reader's eyes move along each line of text without dropping to the lines below. Da Spira's type was also taller, lighter, and more regular than Sweynheym and Pannartz's roman type.

Da Spira's type is one of the most important typefaces ever cut. Almost all of the typefaces designed since 1470, including the one you are reading, have been refinements of his roman type.

Italic Type

Besides being easier to read than Gothic type, roman type also took up less room on the page. Printers who used roman type were able to fit more text on each page, reducing the number of pages required for each book. This compactness made books less expensive to print. As a result, printers could charge less money for their books and therefore sell more.

One of the first printers to recognize the value of smaller, cheaper books was Teobaldo Mannucci of Venice. A scholar of Greek and Latin, Mannucci went by the Latin version of his name, Aldus Manutius, or simply Aldus. His Aldine Press published dozens of ancient Greek and Latin texts between 1493 and 1515 and became the most famous publishing house in the world.

Around 1500, Aldus commissioned Francesco Griffo of Bologna to create an even smaller, more compact version of roman type. Aldus's goal was to produce books that could "more conveniently be held in hand and learned by heart"—the first pocket editions.

Griffo modeled his new type after the handwriting style known as Chancery script. The letters of this script were more slanted and curved than traditional roman type, and they fit very closely together.

Aldus was delighted with the new type and used it for many of his books, beginning in 1501 with a book by the Latin poet Virgil. The Venetian senate granted Aldus a patent on the invention, meaning that other printers were supposed to get permission from Aldus before using this type design. But many other printers, including Griffo himself, used the new type style without bothering to get Aldus's permission. Because this type first appeared in Italy, it became known as italic type.

Type Standardization

As the number of type designs grew, printers began to form ideas about which types worked best and why. Some of these printers published their ideas in books. But as printers tried to communicate about type, they encountered a major problem. Everyone's type was different. Many printers made up names to describe the styles and sizes of their types, but no two printers used the same system. Finally, a French printer named Pierre Fournier decided to measure and categorize type so that it would be easier to discuss and duplicate.

In 1764, Fournier published a guide to typefounding and design entitled *Manuael Typographique*. In this book, Fournier described a method of classifying type by size. He noticed that six lines of type took up about one inch on a page, so he divided an inch into six parts called "lines." To measure the height of a single letter, he divided each line into twelve equal parts called points. This system became known as the point system.

A century after Fournier, American typefounders began to experiment with casting and cutting type by machine. As the number of inventions grew, the United States Founders Association decided to standardize American type with a point system similar to Fournier's. The system devised by the association is still used by American printers and publishers today.

Book Illustration

While some of the early printers tried to make their books more appealing by concentrating on the type they used, others took a different approach. They knew that the illuminated manuscripts of the Middle Ages included artwork, as did many popular block-printed books. As a result, they decided to add pic-

tures to the books they printed with type. In doing so, they invented easier and better ways to include illustrations.

Woodcuts

The first European publisher to include illustrations in a book printed with movable type was also the first one to print a book in the vernacular: Albrecht Pfister. In fact, both "firsts" occurred in the same book, *Edelstein*, by Ulrich Boner, published in 1461. Like most printed art of the Middle Ages, Pfister's illustrations were woodcuts. This posed a problem for the printer, however. The wooden blocks used to print the illus-

This page from Lactantius's Opera *shows the roman type of Sweynheym and Pannartz.*

effe fenfum femiral quericur. tanq̃ illi ad cogitandum rheda & quadrigif opuf eẽt. Democrituf quafi in puteo quodam fic alto ut fundu̓ fit nulluf: uericatem tacere demerfam nimirum ftulce et cetera. Non enim tanq̃ in puteo demerfa eft uericaf: quo uel defcendere uel etiam cadere illi licebat. fed tanq̃ in fũmo montif excelfi uertice: uel potiuf in celo quod eft ueriffimũ. Quid enim eft cur eã potiuf in imũ depreffam diceret: ã̃ f fummũ leuatam nifi forte mente quoq; in pedibuf aut in imif calcibuf cõftituere malebar. potiuf ã̃ in pectore aut f capite? Adeo rẽotiffimi fue/ rũt ab ea uericate: ut eof ne ftatuf qdem fui corpif admoneret: uericatem illif in fummo effe querendam. Ex bac defperatione confeffio illa Socratif nata eft: qua fe nihil fcire dixit nifi hoc unum. q̃ nihil fciat. Hinc achademie difciplĩa manauit. fi tamẽ difciplina dici poteft. in qua ignoratio et difcit et docetur. Sed ne illi quidem qui fcientiam fibi affumpferunt: id ipfum quod fe fcire putabat conftanter defẽdere potuerũt. Qui quonĩa ratio illif non quadrabat: per ignorãtiam rerum diuinarum tã uarii tam incerti fuerunt. fibiq; fepe contraria differentef: ut quid fẽ/ rirent quid uellent: fatif ftatuere ac diiudicare non poffet. Quid igitur pugnef aduerfuf hominef eof: qui fuo fibi gladio pereũt? Quid laboref ut eof deftruaf: quof fua ipfof deftruit atq; afficit oratio? Ariftotelef ingt Cicero ueteref philofophof accufanf eof aut gloriofiffimof aut ftultiffimof fuiffe: q̃ exiftiauiffent phiam fui ingenii effe perfectam. fed fe uidere q̃ pauci annif magna acceffio facta eẽt: breui tempore phiam plane abfolutam fore. Quod ig̃t fuit illud tẽpuf? Quo in oré? Quãdo eft. aut a qbuf abfoluta? Nam q̃ ait ftultiffimof fuiffe q̃ putauiffent ingenii fui perfectam effe fapientiam: uerum eft. fed ne ipfe qdam fatif prudenter: qui aut a ueteribuf ceptam: aut a nouif au ctam: aut mox a pofterioribuf perfectum in putauit. Nunq̃ enim poteft inueftigari. quod non per uiam fuam queritur.

Capitulũ. xxix. Item repetitio de fortuna et natura eiuf & diffinitione eiuf.

Ed repetamuf id quod omifimuf. Fortuna ergo nihil per fe eft. tanq̃ nec fic habendũ eft: tanq̃ fit in aliquo fenfu. Si qdem fortuna é accidẽtium rerũ fubitu̓ atq; inopinatuf euẽtuf. Verum philofophi ne aliquãdo non arrentin re ftultea uolunt trations were a different height than the metal type. As a result, Pfister could not print the illustrations at the same time as the text. His only choice was to print each sheet twice, once with the text and once with the illustration.

In the years that followed, many other publishers also included woodcuts in their books. In France, artists used woodcuts to decorate prayer books known as Books of Hours. In 1498, Philippe Pigouchet produced a Book of Hours that remains one of the most beautiful books ever printed.

That same year, one of the great masterpieces of Western art was created for a book published in Nuremberg, Germany, by Anton Koberger. The book was entitled *Apocalypse.* The artist was Albrecht Dürer. For many, Dürer's woodcut of the *Four Horsemen of the Apocalypse*

Dürer's woodcut, Four Horsemen of the Apocalypse, *is considered one of the great masterpieces of Western art.*

represents the high point of this important art form.

Dürer and Pigouchet were not the only fine artists drawn to the rapidly growing business of printing books. In 1522, Lucas Cranach of Germany provided woodcuts for Martin Luther's best-selling translation of the New Testament. And Hans Holbein created two series of woodcuts for books printed in 1538.

Engravings

Although many fine works were printed with wooden blocks, some artists were dissatisfied with the limited effects. Just as block printers had found it difficult to carve small letters in wood, so too

Albrecht Dürer was one prominent artist whose works were featured in early printed books.

did artists find it difficult to cut lines fine enough for their drawings. As early as 1430, some artists turned to metal to print their art.

In one sense, making a printable design in metal is the opposite of creating one in wood. With a woodcut, the drawing is made on a plank of wood, and the blank areas are carved away. Because the lines of the original drawing stand out in relief from the rest of the wood, this process is known as relief printing. With metal, the lines of the drawing are cut into the plate, and the

Wood engravings like this one depicting a scene from Huckleberry Finn, *are made by carving away the blank areas of a drawing.*

A seventeenth-century engraver works on a book.

blank areas remain flat. This process is known as intaglio printing, or engraving.

To print with an engraved plate, the printer covers the entire plate with ink, then wipes the surface clean. Some of the ink remains in the carved grooves until the plate is pressed against a sheet of paper. The printer uses so much pressure that the paper is actually forced up and into the inked grooves.

With intaglio printing, shallow scratches in the plate hold very little ink while deep grooves hold much more. As a result, an engraver can vary the thickness of the printed lines more than a woodcutter can.

Although engraving allowed artists to draw finer lines than woodcutting did, this process, too, had limitations. Because every groove in the plate was created with the tip of a burin, or steel needle, every engraving consisted of lines and dots. Artists could not blend light and dark areas smoothly, as they could with paint. But innovative artists soon found ways to change that situation.

Mezzotints

One way to soften the lines of an engraving was to change the tool used to cut into the surface. This is what a German artist named Ludwig von Siegen did in 1641. Instead of carefully cutting lines into the plate with a burin, he scratched the surface with serrated rollers and abrasive rockers. This made the surface rough and therefore able to hold ink. Von Siegen then smoothed out certain areas of the plate so they would hold less ink and print lighter. Using this technique, known as mezzotint, von Siegen was able to create soft-edged images that resembled paintings.

In this example of a mezzotint, the artist is able to create a painting-like effect by using soft-edged images.

Etching

Another way to prepare the surface of the printing plate so that it will hold ink is to expose it to a metal-dissolving acid, a process known as etching. The acid eats away a bit of the surface so that it will hold ink. Although no one realized it at the time, the invention of etching was a very important step in the development of the printing press. For the first time in history, chemicals were used to prepare a surface for printing. Knowledge of this process eventually would lead to the invention of photography as well as to the development of presses that would print words without the use of movable type.

To make an etching, the artist first coats the printing plate with soot from a candle or oil lamp. Next, the artist covers the plate with a clear, acid-resisting coating known as a ground. Using steel needles, scrapers, and burnishers,

Rembrandt Van Rijn, one of the first artists to experiment with etching used that technique in this self-portrait.

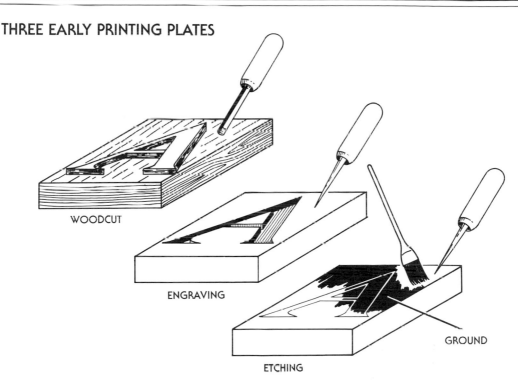

THREE EARLY PRINTING PLATES

WOODCUT

ENGRAVING

ETCHING

GROUND

WOODCUTS

A woodcut plate is made with the method introduced by the Chinese over a thousand years ago. On a woodcut plate, the images to be printed are *raised above* the rest of the plate.

ENGRAVINGS

On an engraved metal plate, invented around 1430, the images to be printed are engraved into the plate. They appear as a series of shallow grooves. To print using an engraved plate, a printer presses the paper against the plate so hard that the paper is actually forced up into the inked grooves.

ETCHINGS

Etching was first used by artists as a way to print detailed drawings. Instead of engraving onto a metal plate, the artist coated the plate with a layer of an acid-resisting "ground." Then the artist scratched, or etched, away the soot-ground compound, exposing the metal wherever he wanted ink to print. When finished, the plate was dipped into an acid bath, which ate away the metal only in those places where it had been etched. Then the plate could be cleaned and used for printing, just like an engraved plate.

the artist removes part of the ground and soot, exposing the metal below. The image appears as light areas against the dark background. The artist then dips the plate in an acid bath. The acid eats

away at the exposed metal until the etched areas are bitten deeply enough to hold ink. When the process is complete, the plate is cleaned and inked for printing.

One of the first artists to experiment with etching was Rembrandt van Rijn of the Netherlands. Although woodcuts and engravings of Rembrandt's work were produced by other artists, etching is the only printing technique Rembrandt himself used.

Refinements in the Press

As printed materials grew in popularity, the need for additional printing presses also grew. Many workshops sought to improve upon Gutenberg's design.

One of the first things printers wanted to improve was the screw that moved the platen up and down. In 1550, a press builder in Nuremberg replaced the wooden screw with a metal one. This made the press both easier to turn and more stable as the paper was pressed against the printing bed.

The next effort to improve the press also involved the screw. This time the concern was not what the screw was made of but how long it took to raise and lower the platen. In 1620, William Blaeu of the Netherlands created a spring-release mechanism that allowed the printer to raise the platen quickly. With this simple change, the number of sheets printed in an hour rose from about fifty to nearly three hundred.

As casting and metal-working methods improved, more metal printing press parts were designed to replace wooden ones. A London, England printing office was the first to use an all-metal press, like this one, in 1800.

est stress. In England, Charles, the Earl of Stanhope, went even further. He used metal to make not only the working parts of his press but also its frame. This first all-metal press was used by the Boydell and Nicol Shakespeare Printing Office in London beginning in 1800.

All-Metal Press

As methods of casting and working metal improved, more and more metal parts were designed to replace wooden ones in the printing press. By 1772, Wilhelm Haas of Basel had designed a press that used metal to make the parts of the press that underwent the great-

The Cylinder Press

While Stanhope was working on the all-iron press, another Englishman was hard at work trying to perfect a design he had first patented in 1790. That man was William Nicholson. His design replaced the flat platen with a three-sided cylinder. Instead of placing the

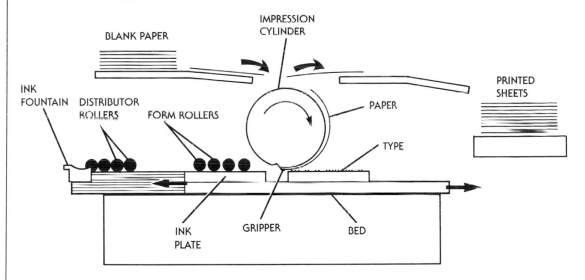

CYLINDER PRESS

BLANK PAPER

IMPRESSION CYLINDER

INK FOUNTAIN

DISTRIBUTOR ROLLERS

FORM ROLLERS

PRINTED SHEETS

PAPER

TYPE

INK PLATE

GRIPPER

BED

The first steam-powered cylinder press was used in 1814. It could print about 1,000 sheets of paper per hour. In this kind of press, the type is placed on a flat bed, which moves back and forth under a rotating cylinder. As the cylinder rotates, a sheet of paper is fed to it and held by a set of steel clamps, known as grippers. As the flat bed moves one direction, the cylinder is raised so that ink can be applied to the type. As the bed moves back the other way, the cylinder is lowered so that the paper comes into contact with the inked type. Then the printed sheet is released from the cylinder and the process begins with a new sheet.

paper in a frame above the type, Nicholson attached a separate sheet of paper to each side of his cylinder. The cylinder moved up and down, like a platen, pressing the paper against the type. The cylinder also rotated. After one sheet of paper was printed, the cylinder turned, positioning another sheet of paper above the type. Meanwhile, one press operator removed the printed sheet from one side of the cylinder, and a second press operator attached a fresh sheet of paper to the other. This design, known as the stop-cylinder press, would soon become the fastest printing press in the world.

Nicholson, however, did not succeed in building this fantastic machine himself. The man who did was Frederick Konig.

Steam-Powered Press

About the time that Nicholson was working on his stop-cylinder press, inventors around the world were starting to use steam engines to power all kinds of machines. One such inventor was Frederick Konig of Suhler, Germany. His idea was to build a printing press powered by steam, but none of his experiments worked. Around 1810, Konig

Visitors view a printing press during an American graphics exhibition in 1876.

traveled to London, where he became familiar with Nicholson's stop-cylinder press. Using this design, Konig built the first successful cylinder press in 1812. Konig's press printed up to eight hundred sheets per hour.

Two years later, Konig produced a second, steam-powered press. This de-

Playwright Alois Senefelder searched for a way to print his own unpublished plays. In the process, he discovered a technique that would make Gutenberg's movable type obsolete.

sign included two cylinders and a movable press bed. While one cylinder pressed down on the bed, the press operators changed the paper in the other. When the first cylinder was finished printing, it rose and the press bed moved beneath the second cylinder. While paper in the first cylinder was changed, the second cylinder printed. This press was capable of producing eleven hundred sheets an hour. In November 1814, it began to be used to print the *London Times*.

More than 350 years after its introduction, Gutenberg's movable type was still being used to print the world's books, pamphlets, and newspapers. The printing press itself had changed, but the process of lowering a sheet of paper onto a bed of raised type had not. Movable type had changed the world, but the world had yet to change movable type.

But a process had already been discovered that would soon make Gutenberg's metal type obsolete. The development of this new process was the work not of a professional printer but of an amateur playwright named Alois Senefelder.

■ ■ ■ ■ ■ ■ ■ ■ ■ CHAPTER **7**

Printing Without Type

By the age of twenty-five, Alois Senefelder had written several plays. Although none of them had been produced or published, Senefelder was certain of their merit. He wanted to bring his plays to the attention of the world, even if he had to print them himself. In 1796, he decided to do just that.

A young, unknown artist, Senefelder did not have much money. He could not afford to pay a printer to publish his plays, nor could he afford to buy metal type. Senefelder knew something about the process of etching, however. He bought a copper plate, prepared it for etching, and began to scratch his words into its surface. When he was done, he placed the plate in an acid bath until the plate was bitten. The first page of his first play was ready for printing.

Senefelder did not mind the long hours spent copying his works onto copper plates, but he did mind the cost. He soon realized that he would not be able to afford enough copper plates to print even one of his plays. He began to look around for another material to use for making printing plates. A native of Bavaria, Senefelder knew that the land around his home contained many flat stones. If he could find a way to etch stone, he would have a plentiful supply of printing plates. He decided to try.

Senefelder's experiment worked. He found the right mixture of chemicals to dissolve the stone, and he was able to

Following his experiments with copper and stone etching, Senefelder discovered he could print using only a stone and a crayon. Pictured here is the title decoration for Senefelder's Treatise on the Invention of Lithography.

print his words clearly. He had one problem, however. Tiny amounts of ink seeped into the porous stone. As a result, the stone transferred small amounts of ink onto areas of the page that were supposed to remain blank.

Knowing that water and oil do not mix, Senefelder decided to try dampening his stone with water before he covered it with the oily ink. He reasoned that the pores in the stone would fill with water and would repel the ink. The etched areas would be deep enough to hold the ink, however, and would print clearly. Senefelder's idea worked. The water retained by the stone repelled the ink completely. In fact, the process worked so well that it gave Senefelder another idea.

Senefelder reasoned that if he could keep water off certain areas of the stone, these "dry" areas would hold ink. If they would hold ink, they would print clearly. In other words, he might be able to use a stone to print without even etching it. He would simply have to treat the surface with something that would block out the water and hold the ink. The answer was readily at hand. Any kind of grease—lard, wax, or even butter—would work.

Senefelder tried a waxy crayon. He drew on a printing stone with the crayon, dampened the stone with water, then covered the surface with ink. The damp areas of the stone repelled the ink, while the areas where he had written with the greasy crayon held it. When Senefelder pressed a sheet of paper against the surface, the ink on the crayoned areas transferred to the paper. Imagine the excitement of the young writer as he found that he could print his plays using nothing more than a stone and a crayon.

Lithography

The process Senefelder invented is called lithography, from the Greek words *lithos,* meaning "stone," and *graphos,* meaning "to write." It was the first printing method ever devised that allowed a printer to transfer ink onto paper using a flat printing plate, a process known as planographic printing.

Before lithography, all printed images in history—from figures of the Buddha block printed by priests in the seventh century to scenes etched by Rembrandt in the seventeenth century—had been created with uneven printing surfaces. The ink was transferred onto the page either from a raised surface, like metal type, or from a recessed surface, like the groove in an engraving. After the discovery of lithography, Senefelder and other printers experimented with different methods of planographic printing. Eventually, most printed materials would be produced using planographic printing methods.

Within two years, Senefelder developed a special press that used stone printing plates. In 1800, Senefelder traveled to England to patent the invention. Three years later, Senefelder found a way to apply his methods to printing with metal plates.

By controlling a flat, metal printing surface with chemicals, Senefelder provided the theoretical basis for printing without raised type. It would take more than a century for Senefelder's idea to be fully developed, but the young writer's discovery was destined to make Gutenberg's greatest breakthrough— the invention of movable metal type— nearly obsolete.

Senefelder' first press, shown here, used stone printing plates. He later replaced stone with metal.

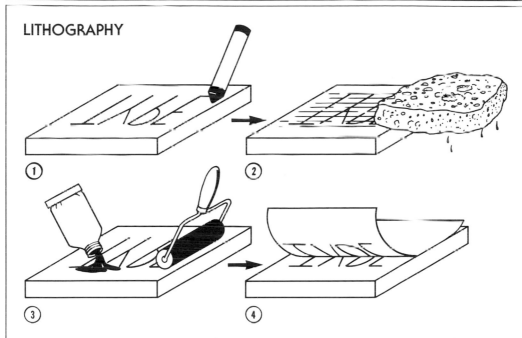

LITHOGRAPHY

Lithography was the first form of printing to use a flat printing plate, with no raised, engraved, or etched images. The image to be printed is simply marked on the plate with wax or another ink-asorbing material (1).

Then the plate is covered with water or another ink-repellant coating that will not cover the wax (2). When ink Is applied to the plate (3), it adheres only to the waxed areas, and only these areas print (4).

Before metal type could be replaced by planographic printing, however, a method had to be found for arranging letters on the printing plate, something other than writing them by hand with a crayon. As with lithography, the solution to this problem involved treating metal plates with chemicals. This discovery, too, occurred far from any print shop, in the separate laboratories of Louis Daguerre and W. H. Fox Talbot.

Photography

In 1835, Daguerre and Talbot were hard at work on one of the most important inventions of the nineteenth century: photography. They both knew that certain chemicals called silver salts turned black when exposed to light. Each inventor used this knowledge to create permanent images with silver salts. Working separately, Talbot and Daguerre each coated small plates, known as photographic plates, with light-sensitive chemicals. Each inventor placed a plate inside a crude version of a camera, a box with a single hole to let in light. They then aimed the open end of the camera at an object. When the inventor opened the shutter that covered the hole, available light reflected from the object and entered the box, passing through a glass lens. The lens focused the light onto the photographic plate. The light caused chemicals on the pho-

Louis Daguerre, pictured in this 1850 woodcut, was one of the two men who found that brief exposure to light would create permanent images on metal plates coated with silver salts.

tographic plate to change color, depending on the strength of the light. The strongest light made the chemicals leave a dark impression on the plate. The weakest light made the chemicals leave a lighter impression. When light reflect-ed from an object like an apple struck the plate, the chemicals changed color in the exact shape as the apple. As a result, an image of the apple appeared on the photographic plate. This image was called a photograph, from the Greek words *photo,* which means "light," and *graphos,* which means "to write."

In 1839, a French inventor named Ponton used the process discovered by Daguerre and Talbot to create metal printing plates. Instead of using silver salts, Ponton coated copper and zinc plates with an acid-resisting chemical known as potassium bichromate. After the plate was exposed to light, it was placed in a acid bath until the image was bitten, like an etching. This process became known as photoengraving because light was used to engrave the plates. This process created very clear images, but it was very costly. Talbot pioneered a way of preparing a plate for printing using the principles of lithography, but this process of photolithography was also expensive.

In 1852, Talbot discovered another way of making a printing plate using photography. He placed a piece of gauze between a photograph and a

The picture of Daguerre on the left is composed of tiny black and white dots clustered together, which can be seen in the close up on the right.

PHOTOENGRAVING

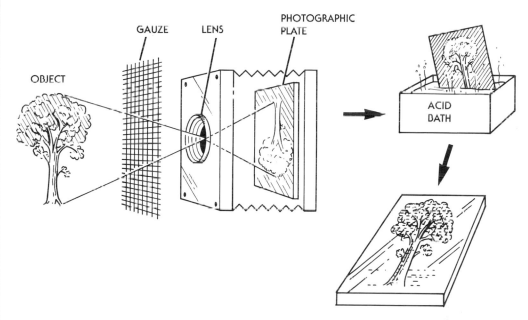

OBJECT

GAUZE LENS PHOTOGRAPHIC PLATE

ACID BATH

The photoengraving method invented by Talbot in 1852 focuses light that passes through a lens onto a metal plate. The plate is covered with an acid-resisting chemical, just like an etching. In this process, however, the chemical is not etched away by hand; it is dissolved by the light. Talbot placed a gauze screen between the lens and the photographed object. This screen breaks the light into a fine pattern of dots, called a halftone. The chemical coating on the plate is dissolved in the same dot pattern. When the plate is dipped into an acid bath, the acid eats away the metal in the same pattern to create the photoengraved plate.

photoengraving plate. The gauze screen broke the light reflected from the photograph into a pattern of dots, known as a halftone. The darkest portions of the image were composed of many black dots clustered together so that they appeared black. The lightest portions of the image were composed of small black and white dots clustered together so that they appeared gray or white. Since the image was made up of nothing more than black and white dots, it was easy to duplicate with black ink on white paper. The photoengrav-

ing plate did not have to record fine shades of gray, so it did not have to be treated with expensive chemicals. Halftones made the printing of photographs affordable for inexpensive publications like magazines and newspapers. In 1880, the first halftone engraving published in a newspaper appeared in the *Daily Graphic* of New York.

The Rotary Press

By the 1800s, newspapers were being purchased by large numbers of people.

Because of their growing business, newspaper publishers had the money to experiment with improvements in the printing press. They also had the need to print more information faster than ever before. As a result, newspapers played an important role in the development of the printing press. The *London Times* purchased the world's first steam-powered press from Frederick Konig in 1812. This machine was soon replaced by even larger and faster presses developed especially for newspaper printing.

In 1845, an American printer named Richard Hoe changed the design of Konig's press in a very important way. Instead of placing the raised type on a flat bed beneath a rotating cylinder, Hoe wrapped the type around the cylinder itself. In addition, Hoe made his cylinder round, instead of three-sided. The cylinder transferred ink onto sheets of paper by rolling against them. Because of its rotating action, Hoe's press became known as the rotary press. It was the first press in the history of the world that did not print with a flat bed of type.

Because Hoe's cylinder rotated, the paper it printed on had to turn along with it to keep from being smeared. Hoe designed his press so that rotating bars, called rollers, moved the paper against the turning cylinder. Since each roller was much smaller than the cylinder, Hoe was able to place several rollers in contact with the cylinder at once. Hoe placed an ink roller between each paper roller so that the type on the cylinder would be properly inked as it came in contact with the paper.

Hoe's cylinder press was a mechanical monster compared to Konig's flat-bed press. It stood three stories high and required no less than ten press operators, but it produced more than two thousand sheets per hour.

The Web Press

The next major advance in press design also occurred in the United States. In 1856, an inventor named William Bullock brought together two ideas to create the fastest printing press in the world. He combined Hoe's cylinder press and a method of making paper developed by a French inventor named Louis Robert. In 1798, Robert had created a machine for making paper in a continuous roll, known as a web, instead of in separate sheets. Bullock designed a rotary press that printed on rolls of paper. This press is known as a web press.

In Bullock's design, the web of paper was fed between two rotating cylinders. One cylinder printed one side of the paper, and the other cylinder printed the other side. After the paper was printed, it was cut into sheets. This press is much faster than one that prints separate sheets, known as a sheet-fed press. Bullock's web press printed and cut up to fifteen thousand sheets per hour. With this design, Bullock was able to print in forty minutes the same number of pages it would have taken Gutenberg two hundred days to produce on his press or Vespansio da Bisticci's fifty scribes twenty-two months to copy by hand.

Color Processing

From the very beginning, printers developed several ways of printing with different colors of ink. For example, in the second book ever printed with mov-

HOE'S ROTARY PRESS

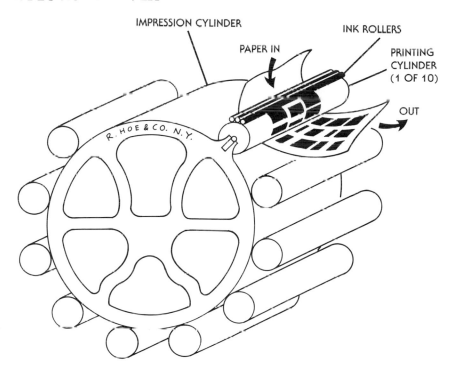

IMPRESSION CYLINDER

PAPER IN

INK ROLLERS

PRINTING CYLINDER (1 OF 10)

OUT

R. HOE & CO. N.Y.

Hoe's rotary press was built in 1847. On the rotary press, type is mounted directly on printing cylinders. Hoe's press had ten cylinders all driven by one large impression cylinder about six feet in diameter. Each printing cylinder had its own inking rollers and could print a different form, so the press could print ten different pages at a time. Modern rotary presses print from 5,000 to 25,000 sheets per hour.

able type, the *Mainz Psalter*, John Fust and Peter Schöffer printed the text in black and the large initials in blue and red. The ink had to be applied to the initials separately in what was a very slow process. Other methods of color printing were also time-consuming. For example, to print a woodcut, engraving, or lithograph with four different colors of ink, each page had to be printed four separate times. The page had to dry between each printing, or the different colors of inks would mix, or bleed, with each other.

In 1893, printers discovered a way of printing color photographs. This required printers to be able to print several different colors of ink at once, without the ink bleeding. They did it by using a process similar to halftone processing. The new process, known simply as color processing, also used a screen to break a photographed image into a pattern of dots, only this time by color. These dots, were smaller than halftone dots. They were so small that different colored dots could be printed side by side without touching and mixing.

The four-color process. Here, the four different color screens of black, magenta, yellow, and cyan are shown. When combined, they form a rosette pattern of dots to form the four-color picture.

They were so close together that the human eye could not separate them. Instead of seeing many dots of different colors, the viewer saw a single image with just a few shades of color.

Color processing is based on the fact that all colors can be grouped into three basic categories: red, green, and blue. To reproduce color on paper, the printer arranges dots of these three basic colors on the page in a way that tricks the eye into seeing many different colors.

Using three different filters, the printer makes three separate photographic negatives. One filter screens out all red, recording a mixture of green and blue known as cyan. Another filter screens out all the green, recording a mixture of red and blue known as magenta. The third filter screens out all the blue, recording a mixture of red and green. When red and green light are mixed, the result is yellow.

By printing dots of cyan, magenta, and yellow closely together, the printer is able to create the illusion of a full-color picture. A fourth color, black, is added to the process to fill in the shadows and create more contrast in the reproduction. For this reason, full-color printing is known as four-color processing. Special presses were developed to print four-color images. These presses use four separate printing plates—one for each color. As the paper passes through the press, each plate prints a dot pattern in a separate color. The halftone screens are arranged so that the dots of ink do not touch and mix. These presses are called four-color presses.

Many press manufacturers add additional plates so that fifth and sixth colors can be printed in one pass through the press. For example, if you wanted to print a metallic gold border around a four-color picture, you could do it in one pass with a five-color press. Often the sixth color printed on a six-color press is not really a color but a clear varnish.

Phototypesetting

Using photographic negatives, printers in the 1890s were able to reproduce all kinds of images—black-and-white and even color—using photographic printing plates. In theory, even a typeset page could be printed without raised type. A printed page could be photographed, then reproduced using photoengraving or photolithography. But raised metal type still had to be used to create the original typeset page. True photographic typesetting would not be possible until the light bulb was invented.

Photographic typesetting is a very simple process. The only things needed are light, film, and a kind of stencil. Light that shines through the stencil will expose the film in the stencil's shape. If the stencil is in the shape of a letter, that letter will appear on the film. If the film is moved and stencils of different letters are used, an entire word, line, or page of text can be made to appear in the correct order on the film.

Nineteenth-century printers had everything they needed for phototypesetting except for a reliable, consistent, and inexpensive source of light. Once Thomas Edison invented the light bulb in 1879, phototypesetting became practical.

The first phototypesetting machine appeared in England in the 1920s, but the process did not come into general use until after World War II. The Foto-

PHOTOTYPESETTING

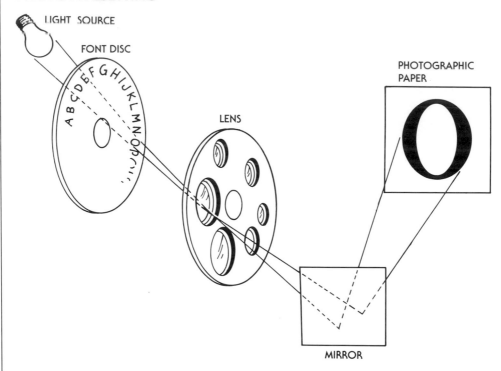

LIGHT SOURCE

FONT DISC

PHOTOGRAPHIC PAPER

LENS

A B C D E F G H I J K L M N O P

MIRROR

Photographic typesetting is a simple application of photography. Light from a light source is shone through a special set of stencils, known as a font disk. The light passes through the desired stencil and is focused by a lens onto a movable mirror. This reflects the light onto a film, causing the desired shape to be exposed on the film.

setter, invented in 1950, was the first commercial phototypesetting machine. It was followed in 1954 by the Photon 200B. Today, hundreds of different models of phototypesetting machines are in use around the world.

Phototypesetting replaced metal typesetting for several reasons. One reason was speed. For four hundred years, one of the most time-consuming aspects of producing books and periodicals had been setting the type by hand. Late in the nineteenth century, two machines—the Linotype machine invented by Ottmar Mergenthaler in 1886 and the Monotype machine invented by Tolbert Lanston in 1893—were devised to speed up the process of setting metal type. Both of these machines worked by casting new type as it was needed, then melting the type down and reusing the metal to cast more letters. Although these machines were fast, phototypesetting machines were even faster.

Phototypesetters were also more compact and less expensive to operate than metal typesetting equipment. Mistakes were more easily corrected with film than with metal type. Film also allowed printers to change the size and shape of type as never before. Most phototypesetters included magnifying lenses to enlarge the images formed on the film. Other lenses were used to distort the type, making it more condensed or expanded. Some lenses were created to slant the type or even bend it.

Since type no longer had to be sculpted from metal and then cast, type designers were free to experiment with typographic forms that knew no physical bounds. This has led to an explosion of new typefaces in the twentieth century.

Offset Printing

Phototypesetting was a carefully planned step forward for planographic printing. But another important development came about by sheer accident. Printers knew that when a rotary press ran out of paper, the printing cylinder pressed its ink onto the paper rollers. They noticed that when more paper was fed into the machine, the rollers printed as clearly as the printing cylinder did.

In 1906, two American printers used this knowledge to create planographic presses that were vastly more efficient than standard lithographic presses. One of these men was Ira Rubel of Nutley, New Jersey. The other was A. F. Harris of Niles, Ohio. The process they invented is known as offset printing.

In offset printing, a photoengraved or photolithographic printing plate is prepared as usual. This plate transfers ink to another printing plate, known as the blanket. The blanket then transfers the ink to the paper. The original printing plate never comes into contact with the paper.

The blanket, which is made of rubber, is chemically treated to repel water and attract ink, just like a lithographic stone. Some rollers in the press keep the blanket constantly moist. Other rollers keep it constantly inked. As a result, offset printing is clean and precise. Because the rubber blankets can be used over and over, an offset press is inexpensive to run. Because offset printing is based on the principles of lithography, it is sometimes called offset lithography.

Gravure Printing

Planographic printing, including standard and offset lithography, is the most widely used printing process today. It has made printing with raised surfaces, or relief printing, virtually obsolete. But planographic printing is not the only kind of printing in use. Printing with recessed surfaces, or engravings, is far from dead. In fact, many of the world's largest printing companies use only a special kind of intaglio printing known as gravure.

Gravure printing is a form of photoengraving. The platemaker first fills a metal screen with light-sensitive gelatins known as carbon tissue. When the carbon tissue is exposed to light reflected from a photograph, the areas that receive the most light harden. The areas that receive little light remain soft. The carbon tissue is then placed in a hot water bath to dissolve the gelatins. The hard gelatins dissolve more slowly than the soft ones do, so certain areas of the screen remain thicker than others.

The carbon tissue is then placed on the copper plates and exposed to an acid called ferric chloride for a brief

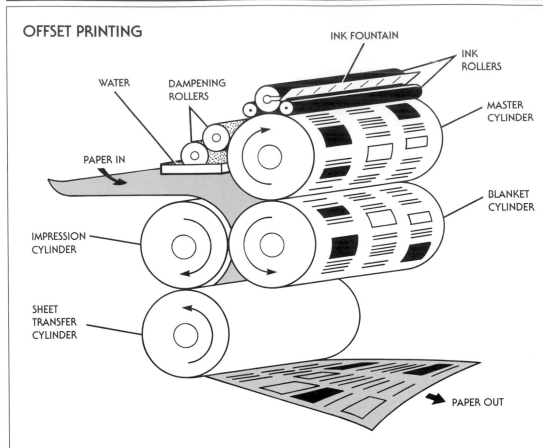

OFFSET PRINTING

INK FOUNTAIN

INK ROLLERS

WATER

DAMPENING ROLLERS

MASTER CYLINDER

PAPER IN

BLANKET CYLINDER

IMPRESSION CYLINDER

SHEET TRANSFER CYLINDER

PAPER OUT

Offset printing is the most common form of printing in use today. It uses the lithographic process, but the original printing plate never comes in contact with the printed paper. Instead, ink is first *offset* from the printing plate to a rubber blanket, and then from the blanket it is printed on paper. The soft, rubber surface of the blanket creates a crisp, precise image.

period of time. The acid eats through the gelatins to the copper plate beneath. Where the carbon tissue is thickest, the acid barely reaches the surface, etching shallow holes that hold very little ink. Where the tissue is thinnest, the acid reaches the surface more quickly and etches deeper holes.

The etched plate is placed around a cylinder for printing. As the cylinder turns, the plate is dipped in a bath of ink and then passed beneath a steel blade, known as the doctor blade. The doctor blade scrapes all the ink off the surface of the plate. The holes in the plate retain different amounts of ink, depending on their size. The larger holes hold more ink, and the smaller ones hold less. As the cylinder continues to turn, the plate comes into contact with the paper. The larger holes print darker, and the small holes print lighter. The final printing, then, corresponds exactly to the original film positive.

The gravure process reproduces continuous tones more precisely than the halftone process does, so it is the preferred method of reproducing photography. Its platemaking process is very expensive, however. As a result, gravure printing is practical only for large press runs. New methods are making gravure printing less costly, but this process is still mainly used for large-volume printing, such as magazines and mail-order catalogs.

Xerography

From the beginning of the nineteenth century to the middle of the twentieth, many things about the printing process changed: how the press was powered, the shape and texture of its printing plates, and how the plates were prepared for printing. Only the basic process of putting ink on paper remained the same. But now, even this has changed.

Beginning in the 1930s, various inventors began to experiment with different forms of dry printing, or xerography. The basic concept is to create a temporary image on a plate, then transfer the image to the paper. One method, known as thermography, uses heat to bond special dry compounds, or toner, to certain areas of the paper. The process that proved most practical, however, is electrophotography. This process was introduced by the Xerox Corporation in 1960.

With electrophotography, an area of the copying machine, called the photoconductor surface, is charged with electricity. When this surface is exposed to light, it loses its charge.

To make a copy, an original image on paper is placed above the photoconductor surface and exposed to light. The blank areas of the original cause portions of the photoconductor surface to lose their charge. The dark areas of the original, however, cause the corresponding parts of the photoconductor surface to retain their charge. These charged areas then attract oppositely charged toner. The toner becomes fixed to the printing paper by heat, pressure, or chemicals.

With xerographic copying machines, or photocopiers, it became easy and affordable to print small numbers of documents instantly. Virtually every business in the industrial world has acquired at least one photocopier.

Xerography is also the technology that has been used to create printers that print out information from computers. When connected to a laser printer, the computer "writes" an image onto a photoconductor surface using a concentrated laser light.

Each day, billions of pages of documents are printed using xerography—without type, without permanent printing plates, and without ink. With xerography, the only thing still left of the ancient printing process is the material that began it all nearly two thousand years ago: Ts'ai Lun's marvelous invention, paper.

Yet in some areas of publishing, even paper is no longer used.

Printing in the Computer Age

Some people who study trends in business and culture have predicted that certain kinds of printing may soon vanish. They believe the printing press will be replaced by the computer and that the printed page will be replaced with an electronic page. To understand this reasoning, we need to think again about the basic uses of printing.

Throughout history, printing has been used for three basic purposes: decoration, communication, and information storage.

Decorative Printing

The first use of printing was decorative. The very first block prints were used to decorate fabric. Today, printing methods are still used to produce patterns on clothing, linens, and furniture. Printing is also used to decorate disposable items such as paper towels, napkins, and tissues. One of the largest uses of printing today is to decorate product packaging—cereal boxes, potato chip bags, can and jar labels, and virtually everything else you see on the shelves of supermarkets and retail stores. In addition, printing is used to produce posters and fine art prints for the decoration of homes, offices, and public buildings.

The role of printing in the decorative arts is not likely to change greatly in the near future. This is because the cost of printing is incredibly low when it is used to produce mass quantities of an item. In most cases, the press runs,

or amount of items printed, for fabric, disposable items, and product packaging are enormous. Hundreds of thousands of yards of fabric are printed with a single design, then shipped to manufacturers all over the world. Millions, even billions, of soup labels, gum wrappers, and milk cartons are printed without any change of design. When such large quantities are needed, no other method of decoration can compete in cost with printing.

Computer-Controlled Presses

That is not to say that computers will not affect decorative printing. They already have. Computers are able to assist printers for the same reason that they have proven helpful in almost every other business: they are able to store and retrieve information. They cannot really think, but they can remember.

For example, a computer attached to a printing press can be told how much ink is needed on the printing plate to produce the best possible image. The same computer can be connected to sensors that measure the flow of ink onto the printing plate. Using its sensors and the information in its memory, the computer can monitor the amount of ink being used, making sure it is the correct amount. Once it is set up, a computer can perform this task more accurately and less expensively than a human press operator can.

Computers can control the amount of ink needed for printing more accurately and less expensively than can a human press operator.

Computer-controlled color separation, shown here, brings clearer and more colorful images to the printed page than ever before.

Similarly, computers can be programmed to control the parts of the press that feed, fold, and cut the paper. The human press operator needs only to change the printing plates, mix and load the ink, and make certain the press does not run out of paper. Should the human being make any mistakes, the computers will stop the press until the error is corrected.

Computerized Page Makeup

Special computers have also been designed to speed up the work that must be done before a printing job can be put on the press. This usually involves typesetting, layout, and platemaking. The computers that help with these tasks all work in the same way. They break up the images into a pattern of dots, store the placement of these dots in their memories, then print the dots in the exact location chosen by the computer operator. This process is known as digitizing.

For typesetting, a computer stores a wide variety of type characters in its

Page layout can be done quickly with computers.

memory as digitized information. As the text is typed into the computerized typesetting machine, the shapes of the letters are retrieved from the computer's memory. When the text is complete, the typesetter commands the computer to print the digitized characters. Using dry toner, the text can be printed directly onto paper. This process is known as laser printing. The text can also be printed onto photographic paper using the basic principles of phototypesetting. Once the text has been printed, it can be arranged by hand just like standard phototypeset text to create a page, a process known as page layout.

Photographs and artwork can be digitized in the same way. Using special sensors and laser light, the computer scans the image and breaks it into a pattern of dots. The computer stores this information until it is needed for printing. The computer can then recreate the digitized image on regular paper or photographic paper.

The process of digitizing also works for the duplication of color images. The laser notes not only the position of each dot but also its color. The color image can then be transferred to clear photographic film or to photographic paper. Some computers are able to transfer digitized images directly onto printing plates. This saves not only time but also the expense of standard platemaking and color separation.

Ink-Jet Printing

Before the invention of computers, all printing done with wet ink had been the result of contact between two surfaces, the inked surface and the paper. Xerography was the only printing process that did not use the contact method to transfer ink to the page. Once the process of digitizing was perfected, however, a process was developed to transfer wet ink to a page without the use of an inked surface. This process is known as ink-jet printing. In this process, a digitized image is stored in a computer's memory. The computer is connected to a bank of very small spraying nozzles. As a piece of paper passes beneath the nozzles, the computer commands the nozzles to spew out dots of ink in exactly the same pattern as that of the stored image in the computer's memory. Since the ink is sprayed onto the paper, no printing plate is needed.

Altering Images by Computer

Computers can do much more than scan and copy an original image. Once a digitized design is stored in the computer's memory, the computer operator can change the image in many ways. In the case of a color photograph, for example, the computer user can darken, brighten, or even change the colors within the picture. This process is known as image enhancement. The image can also be made larger or smaller. The picture can be stretched, turned, or reversed. For example, the publisher of this book recently used a computer to create a panoramic view of the Japanese city of Hiroshima, which was destroyed by the first atom bomb. Two photographs were taken of the city after the bomb had exploded. Placed side by side, the two images almost created a panoramic view of the city. The photographs, however, were taken at slightly different angles, and they did

Using a computer, a modern-day typesetter can manipulate the size and quality of scanned-in art.

not match exactly. The publisher used a computer to align the two photographs to form a single view of the city.

Communication

Ever since Buddhist priests first added words to their block prints in the eighth century, printing has been used to communicate. Unlike decorative printing, printed communication changes frequently. The contents of a newspaper change daily. Each issue of a magazine is completely new. Even books are frequently revised.

The more often printed materials are changed, the more costly they are to produce. As a result, other, cheaper methods of delivering the same information now compete with printing.

A person who has a computer at home, for example, can subscribe to an electronic communication network, such as Prodigy, to receive information, such as daily news, directly into the computer. A person who relies on a computer network for the daily news might choose

Sophisticated laser scanners, like this one, brought printing into the modern age. Technology continues to advance, building on past discoveries and inventions.

to stop subscribing to the newspaper. Eventually, this trend could make printed newspapers obsolete.

Printing also consumes a great deal of natural resources, such as paper, while electronic delivery systems do not. As resources grow more scarce, computer networks might become more popular.

The news is only one form of communication that is now available in electronic form. Puzzles, poetry, short stories, and even novels are stored on computer bulletin boards that can be accessed by phone. The computer user can read this material on the computer screen or even load it into the computer and print it out on paper. A great deal of lit-

The contents of entire books, such as encyclopedias, can now be stored on a compact disk.

erature is now being read that has never been printed on a printing press.

Printed books may even be replaced by computerized books someday. Right now, one of the main advantages printed materials enjoy over electronic communications is portability. A reader does not need to be near an electrical outlet to enjoy a book or magazine. However, pocket-size computers powered by batteries or light have existed for years. A hand-held computer with a page-size screen could be produced with the contents of not just one but dozens of books in its memory. If the same computer could be loaded with new information from an electronic computer network, it could function as a magazine or modern-day newsbook.

The main drawback to computerized books is their readability. A computer screen is harder to read than a printed page. In the future, however, finer screens with greater resolution could duplicate the appearance of the printed page. At that point, computerized books might well replace printed ones.

Information Storage

The first printed books to be replaced by computer systems will probably be reference books and technical manuals.

These books are not read for pleasure or entertainment. Their function is to store information for occasional retrieval. They perform this task well, but computers perform it better. In fact, many reference books—including *Grollier's Encyclopedia* and the *Guide to Periodic Literature*—are now available in electronic formats.

Many publishers make their information available for retrieval by computers. Some publishers sell their data on magnetic disks, known as floppy disks, on magnetic tape, or on compact disks. Others allow their customers to access their data over the phone, just like computer bulletin boards. No matter what the medium, electronic storage and retrieval systems are usually more compact, faster, and less expensive than printed books.

This does not mean that libraries of printed books will disappear. Electronic systems work best when a person needs to look something up. When a person wants to read a great deal about a certain subject—the invention of the printing press, for example—a printed book like this one will most likely continue to be the most portable and least expensive source of information.

Glossary

■ ■

alloy: A mixture of two or more metals.

artisan: A manually skilled worker.

blanket: A rubber mat that transfers a printed image from a printing plate to a sheet of paper in an offset press.

block printing: The process of transferring ink from a carved wooden block onto a sheet of paper or fabric.

broadside: A sheet of paper with text printed on one side.

burin: A tool used for engraving a metal plate.

calligraphy: The art of handwriting.

casting: The process of forming an object, such as a coin, by pouring molten material into a mold and allowing it to harden.

chase: A frame, usually metal, designed to hold individual pieces of type together to form a block of text.

dialect: A version of a language spoken in a particular region.

engraving: The process of printing with a plate that bears a recessed design.

etching: The process of recessing certain areas of a printing plate by exposing them to a chemical bath.

folio: A large sheet of paper, parchment, or vellum, folded once in the middle, making two leaves or four pages of a book or manuscript.

form: Type, space bars, and all other matter locked in a chase for printing.

gravure: A method of printing with photoengraved printing plates.

halftone: A photographic image composed of many dots made by placing a screen between photoengraving plate and the source of light.

illuminated manuscripts: A handwritten text decorated with brightly colored designs and pictures.

index: An alphabetized list usually in the back of a printed work that gives the pages on which various names, places, and subjects occur.

intaglio printing: The process of printing that uses a recessed printing surface.

leading: Bars placed between lines of type to create open space.

lithography: A printing process in which a flat surface, such as a stone or metal plate, is chemically treated so that ink adheres only to the portions that are to be printed.

manuscript: A handwritten composition, such as a book or document.

matrix: A mold into which the design of a letter has been embossed.

metallurgy: The science and technology of metals and their properties.

mezzotint: A design made by printing with a plate that has been scratched with serrated rollers and abrasive rockers.

miniature: A very small painting.

mold: A hollow form into which molten material is poured to be shaped.

movable type: Interchangeable pieces of type that can be arranged to create a block of text.

negative space: The blank areas of a printed page.

news ballad: A news account written in poetic form, often to the rhythm of a popular song.

newsbook: A pamphlet that reports on a single news event.

parchment: An animal skin, usually sheepskin or goatskin, prepared as a material for writing or drawing on.

photocopier: A machine that duplicates a graphic image using electrostatic forces.

photoengraving: The process of engraving a printing plate by exposing light-sensitive materials to light.

photograph: An image produced on a light-sensitive surface, such as a chemically treated sheet of paper.

photography: The process of creating images by briefly exposing chemically treated surfaces to light.

photolithography: The process of creating a lithographic printing plate by exposing light-sensitive chemicals to light.

phototypesetting: The process of transferring the image of type characters onto photographic paper or film to form a block of text.

planographic printing: A printing process that uses a flat printing plate.

platen: A flat metal plate that holds paper against the type in a printing press.

proofread: To look for errors in a text and to mark the corrections to be made.

punch: A tool for embossing a design into a softer material.

relation: A printed news account or narration, a newsbook.

rubbing: An image obtained by placing a sheet of paper over a raised surface and rubbing with a marking substance.

scribe: A person who earns money by copying manuscripts or documents by hand.

scriptorium: The writing room of a monastery where manuscripts are copied.

serif: The short cross-lines or feet, at the bottom of a letter.

silver salt: Light-sensitive chemical, silver iodide.

stamp: To imprint or impress with a small, raised surface.

stencil: A sheet of material, such as paper, into which a design has been cut so that paint or ink applied to the sheet will reproduce the design on the surface beneath.

toner: An imaging material, either wet or dry, used in xerography.

type: small blocks with raised characters that leave an impression when inked and pressed upon a material such as paper.

typesetting: The process of arranging individual pieces of type, either by hand or by computer, to form a block of text.

vellum: An animal skin, usually calfskin, lambskin, or kidskin, prepared for writing or drawing on.

vernacular: The everyday language spoken in a country or region.

web: A continuous roll of printing paper.

web press: A press that prints on a roll of paper rather than on single sheets.

woodcut: A wooden block with a surface carved for printing of a picture or design.

xerography: A process of copying a graphic image by arranging toner on paper using electrostatic forces.

For Further Reading

Clifford Lindsey Alderman, *The Story of the Thirteen Colonies*. New York: Random House, Inc., 1966.

Albert Barker, *Black on White and Read All Over*. New York: J. Messner, 1971.

Dan Bolognese and Robert Thornton, *Drawing and Painting with the Computer*. New York: Franklin Watts, Inc., 1983.

Lorraine Conway, *The Middle Ages*. New York: Good Apple, 1987.

Alice Dalgliesh, *The Fourth of July Story*. New York: Charles Scribner's Sons, 1956.

Alice Dickinson, *The Stamp Act*. New York: Franklin Watts, Inc., 1976.

R. E. Evans, *The American War of Independence*. Minneapolis: Lerner Publications Co., 1977.

Brayton Harris, *Johann Gutenberg and the Invention of Printing*. New York: Franklin Watts, Inc., 1972.

Michael Kronenwetter, *Politics and the Press*. New York: Franklin Watts, Inc., 1987.

Milton Lomask, *The First American Revolution*. New York: Farrar, Straus and Giroux, Inc., 1974.

Fiona MacDonald, *Everyday Life in the Middle Ages*. Morristown, New Jersey: Silver Burdett Company, 1985.

Katherine Marcuse, *The Devil's Workshop*. Nashville: Abingdon Press, 1979.

Douglas McMurtrie, *Wings for Words: The Story of Johann Gutenberg and His Invention of the Printing Press*. New York: Rand McNally, 1940.

Richard B. Morris, *The First Book of the American Revolution*. New York: Franklin Watts, 1956.

Susan B. Pfeffer, *A Matter of Principle*. New York: Delacorte Press, 1982.

Pierre Miguel, *Days of Knights & Castles*. Morristown, New Jersey: Silver Burdett Company, 1985.

Susan Purdy, *Books for You to Make*. New York: Lippincott, 1973.

Donald J. Rogers, *Press Versus Government: Constitutional Issues*. New York: J. Messner, 1986.

Martin W. Sandler, *The Story of American Photography*. New York: Little Brown and Co., Inc., 1979.

R. J. Unstead, *Living in a Medieval Village*. Reading, Massachusetts: Addison-Wesley Publishing Co., Inc., 1971.

Melvyn B. Zerman, *Taking on the Press: Constitutional Rights in Conflict*. New York: Crowell Junior Books, 1986.

Works Consulted

Margaret Aston, *The Fifteenth Century: The Prospect of Europe.* San Diego: Harcourt Brace Jovanovich, Inc., 1968.

Nicolas Barker, *The Oxford University Press and the Spread of Learning, 1478-1978.* Oxford, England: Oxford University Press, 1978.

Daniel J. Boorstin, *The Discoverers.* New York: Vintage Books, 1983.

Thomas Francis Carter, *The Invention of Printing in China and Its Spread Westward.* New York: The Ronald Press Company, revised, 1955.

Warren Chappell, *A Short History of the Printed Word.* New York: Alfred A. Knopf, 1970.

Svend Dahl, *History of the Book.* Metuchen, New Jersey: The Scarecrow Press, Inc., 1968.

Will Durant, *The Reformation.* New York: Simon & Schuster, 1950.

Esther S. Harley and John Hampden, *Books: From Papyrus to Paperback.* New York: Roy Publishers, 1963.

Denys Hay, *Europe in the Fourteenth and Fifteenth Centuries.* London: Longman Group, 1966.

Berthold Laufer, *Paper and Printing in Ancient China.* New York: Burt Franklin, 1931.

S. H. Steinberg, *Five Hundred Years of Printing.* Baltimore: Penguin Books, 1955.

Mitchell Stephens, *A History of News.* New York: Viking Penguin, Inc., 1988.

Alan G. Thomas, *Fine Books.* New York: G. P. Putnam's Sons, 1967.

Index

About the Author

A widely published poet and playwright, Bradley Steffens is the author of five children's books. His fascination with printing began early, when he experimented with printing and publishing at the age of eleven after he received a printing set from his parents.

Picture Credits

■ ■

The Bettmann Archive, 12 (both), 13 (all), 14, 21, 36, 41 (bottom), 47, 49 (both), 50, 52 (bottom), 53, 54 (bottom left), 57, 62 (top left), 63 (left), 69, 70, 72 (all)

Ron Blakeley/Uniphoto Picture Agency, 83 (top right), 85 (top right)

Rick Brady/Uniphoto Picture Agency, 86

The Hulton-Deutsch Collection, 42

The J. Paul Getty Museum, 22, 23 (all), 24 (all)

Library of Congress, 15, 16, 18, 20, 25 (both), 26 (both), 27, 28 (both), 29, 30, 33, 34 (both), 35, 38, 40 (both), 41 (top), 43 (both), 44, 46 (both), 52 (top), 54 (top, bottom right), 55 (both), 61, 62 (top right), 63 (right), 64 (both), 66, 68 (both), 76

National Archives, 58

Joseph L. Paris, 83 (bottom), 85 (left)

Uniphoto Picture Agency, 83, 85, 86

Cover photo: © Dawson Jones/Stock Boston